The International High IC

The International High IQ Society, the second largest high-IQ organization in the world, was founded in New York City by Nathan Haselbauer. He created the society in April 2000 to enable bright people from around the world to come together on the Internet. The society welcomes people from all walks of life who have an IQ in the top five per cent of the world's population and who want to be part of the society's global community. The society is unique in that its combined membership includes people of all ages, races and professions, and literally spans the globe.

The main goals of the society are to foster intellectual thinking and to provide opportunities for our members to socialize with each other. These goals are accomplished through the society's discussion forums, various tournaments, numerous online activities, a quarterly magazine, and functions held throughout the world.

Membership in the International High IQ Society is open to persons who score within the top five per cent of the general population on one of the society's admissions tests. There is no other qualification for membership.

For more information visit www.highiqsociety.org or send an e-mail to membership@highiqsociety.org.

Also available

THE MAMMOTH BOOK OF
NEW
IQ
PUZZLES

Nathan Haselbauer

ROBINSON

RUNNING PRESS
PHILADELPHIA · LONDON

Constable & Robinson Ltd
3 The Lanchesters
162 Fulham Palace Road
London W6 9ER
www.constablerobinson.com

First published in the UK by Robinson,
an imprint of Constable & Robinson, 2010

A copy of the British Library Cataloguing in Publication
Data is available from the British Library

UK ISBN 978-1-84901-004-7

1 3 5 7 9 10 8 6 4 2

First published in the United States in 2010
by Running Press Book Publishers

9 8 7 6 5 4 3 2 1
Digit on the right indicates the number of this printing

US Library of Congress number: 2009929919

US ISBN 978-0-7624-3724-5

Running Press Book Publishers
2300 Chestnut Street
Philadelphia, PA 19103-4371

Visit us on the web!
www.runningpress.com

Printed and bound in the EU

Typesetting and editorial: Basement Press
Proofreading and checking: Puzzle Press

CONTENTS

INTRODUCTION

The aim of the *The Mammoth Book of New IQ Puzzles* is to stretch your mind and to entertain you. As the president and founder of the International High IQ Society, I've been writing, gathering, and solving puzzles for years. I've tried to include some tough challenges in this new book, but there are puzzles that will suit a novice puzzle solver too. The puzzles will exercise your powers of logic, some will require mathematical skills and there are others which also test your general knowledge.

Each puzzle is rated according to its difficulty, ranging from 1 (easy) to 5 (very difficult). The chapters become progressively more difficult: chapter 1 is a selection of relatively simple puzzles and chapter 12 features the most difficult in the book. The difficulty rating or "score" for each chapter is given on the chapter opening page – it represents the sum total of the difficulty ratings for the puzzles contained in the chapter. Answers can be found at the end of each chapter.

Work your way through the book and you will have the satisfaction of trying a whole range of puzzles of differing degrees of difficulty. There's no time limit for any of the puzzles so take as long as you like.

Many of the puzzle books in bookstores today are simply remakes of the old classics. As with all my books, I've made a special effort to design each puzzle with a fresh, innovative approach. I hope you have as much fun solving these puzzles as I had creating them. I would be pleased to hear from puzzle aficionados and welcome any correspondence.

Nathan Haselbauer

DIFFICULTY RATING: 38

WHO WINS?

When Peter and Duncan ran a 100-meter race, Peter won by 5 meters. So to give Duncan a chance they raced again, but this time Peter started 5 meters behind the starting line.

Each man ran the race at the same speed as in the first race.

What were the results of the second race?

ANSWER:

| Puzzle 1.1 | Difficulty rating: 1 |

MISSING WORD

Complete the comparison:

PLANT is to SEED as WINE is to . . .

A. Sun
B. Flower
C. Grape
D. Liquor

ANSWER:

Puzzle 1.2	Difficulty rating: 1

ODD ONE OUT

Which one of these forms does not belong with the rest?

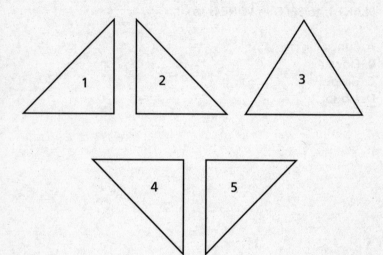

ANSWER:

Puzzle 1.3	Difficulty rating: 1

GUMBALLS

If 1,000 gumballs cost $20, how much would ten gumballs cost?

ANSWER:

| Puzzle 1.4 | Difficulty rating: 1 |

SPATIAL PUZZLE

Which of the following rectangles is on the bottom?

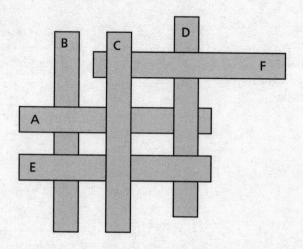

ANSWER:

Puzzle 1.5	Difficulty rating: 1

MISSING WORD

Complete the comparison:

CANADA is to NORTH AMERICA as EGYPT is to . . .

A. Asia
B. Africa
C. Europe
D. Pacific Rim
E. Eurasia

ANSWER:

Puzzle 1.6	Difficulty rating: 1

COMPLETE THE SEQUENCE

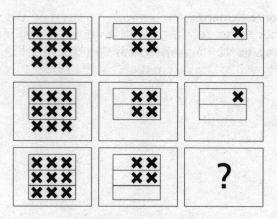

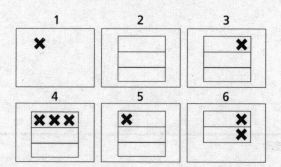

Which one is correct?

ANSWER:

UP A LADDER

Chris is on a ladder painting a wall. He starts on the middle rung, goes up six rungs, goes down eight rungs, up three rungs, and up 12 more rungs to reach the top bar of the ladder. How many rungs are there on the ladder?

ANSWER:

| **Puzzle 1.8** | **Difficulty rating: 1** |

COMPLETE THE SEQUENCE

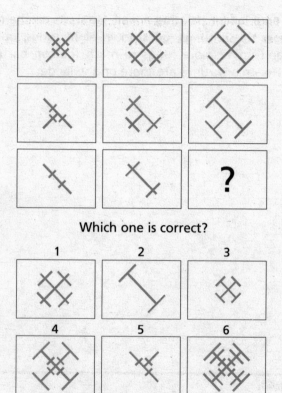

Which one is correct?

1	2	3

4	5	6

ANSWER:

Puzzle 1.9	Difficulty rating: 1

ALPHABET

In the English alphabet, how many letters are there between the letter "i" and the letter "q"?

ANSWER:

| Puzzle 1.10 | Difficulty rating: 1 |

ODD ONE OUT

Which one of these forms does not belong with the rest?

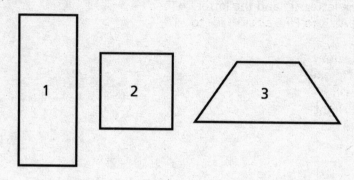

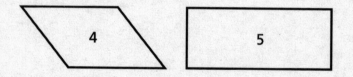

ANSWER:

Puzzle 1.11	Difficulty rating: 1

MISSING WORD

Complete the comparison:

HEAT is to FIRE as LIGHT is to . . .

A. Sun
B. Smoke
C. Dark
D. Night

ANSWER:

Puzzle 1.12	Difficulty rating: 1

WORD PUZZLE

Can the word COMPASS be spelled using only the letters found in the word MICROPROCESSOR?

ANSWER:

| Puzzle 1.13 | Difficulty rating: 1 |

COMPLETE THE SEQUENCE

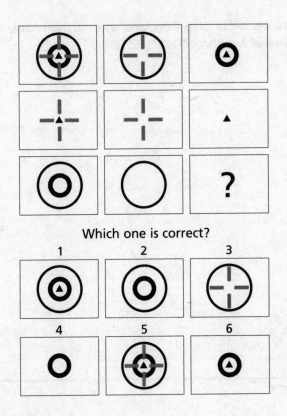

Which one is correct?

1   2   3

4   5   6

ANSWER:

Puzzle 1.14	Difficulty rating: 1

TALLEST

If Duncan is taller than Mick and shorter than Josh, who is the tallest of the three?

ANSWER:

| Puzzle 1.15 | Difficulty rating: 1 |

MISSING WORD

CLARINET is to WOODWIND as TRUMPET is to . . .

A. Musician
B. Brass
C. Instrument
D. Percussion
E. Copper

ANSWER:

Puzzle 1.16	Difficulty rating: 1

DORKS AND XORGS

If most Gannucks are Dorks and most Gannucks are Xorgs, the statement that some Dorks are Xorgs is:

A. True
B. False
C. Indeterminable from data

ANSWER:

| Puzzle 1.17 | Difficulty rating: 1 |

COMPLETE THE SEQUENCE

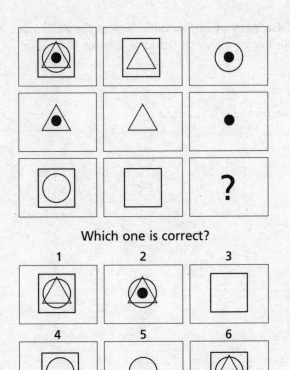

Which one is correct?

1 2 3

4 5 6

ANSWER:

| Puzzle 1.18 | Difficulty rating: 1 |

OLDEST

Danielle is now as old as Kelly was eight years ago. Who is older?

ANSWER:

MISSING WORD

Complete the comparison:

CEYLON is to SRI LANKA as . . . is to ZIMBABWE

A. Abyssinia
B. Rhodesia
C. Africa
D. Harare
E. Swaziland

ANSWER:

Puzzle 1.20	Difficulty rating: 1

WORD PUZZLE

Can the word SKATES be spelled by using the first letters of the words in the following sentence: Should kids attempt selling egg shells?

ANSWER:

| Puzzle 1.21 | Difficulty rating: 1 |

NUMBER SEQUENCE

Which of the following numbers doesn't fit the sequence?

13 18 14 19 15 21 16

ANSWER:

| Puzzle 1.22 | Difficulty rating: 1 |

COMPLETE THE SEQUENCE

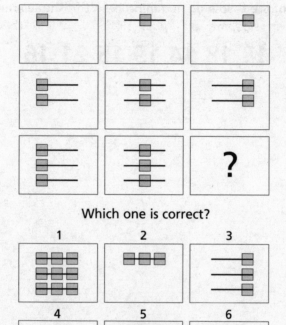

Which one is correct?

1   2   3

4   5   6

ANSWER:

Puzzle 1.23 | Difficulty rating: 1

TAKE A NAP

During naptime Josh was sleeping between Jimmy and Paul. Andy was sleeping on Paul's right (assuming they are visualised sleeping head down). Who was Paul sleeping between?

ANSWER:

| Puzzle 1.24 | Difficulty rating: 1 |

MISSING WORD

Complete the comparison:

SUFFOCATION is to AIR as STARVATION is to . . .

A. Water
B. Food
C. Anorexia
D. Death

ANSWER:

Puzzle 1.25	Difficulty rating: 1

LIKE FORMS

The first four forms are alike in a certain way. Pick the numbered form that is also alike.

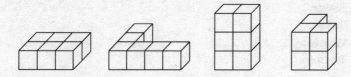

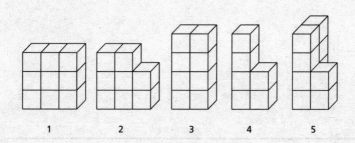

1   2   3   4   5

ANSWER:

| Puzzle 1.26 | Difficulty rating: 1 |

MISSING WORD

Complete the comparison:

SLICE is to LOAF as INGREDIENT is to . . .

A. Bread
B. Bake
C. Whole
D. Recipe

ANSWER:

| Puzzle 1.27 | Difficulty rating: 1 |

COMPLETE THE SEQUENCE

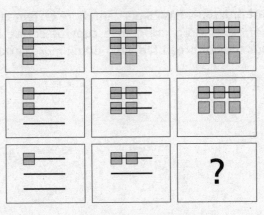

Which one is correct?

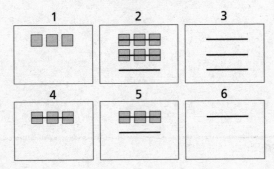

ANSWER:

| Puzzle 1.28 | Difficulty rating: 1 |

CAFFEINE HIGH

One cup of green tea has 25 per cent more caffeine than one cup of coffee. If Greg drinks five cups of coffee and Tim drinks four cups of green tea, who drank more caffeine?

ANSWER:

| Puzzle 1.29 | Difficulty rating: 1 |

MISSING WORD

Complete the comparison:

GUM is to CHEW as BOOK is to . . .

A. Read
B. Paper
C. Cover
D. Author
E. Recipes

ANSWER:

| Puzzle 1.30 | Difficulty rating: 1 |

COMPLETE THE SEQUENCE

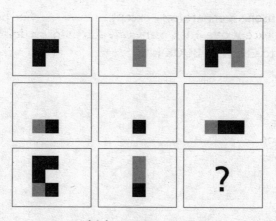

Which one is correct?

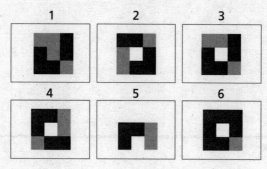

CATS AND GOLDFISH

All of Alison's pets are cats except one. All of her pets are goldfish except one. How many cats and goldfish does Alison have?

ANSWER:

Puzzle 1.32	Difficulty rating: 1

MISSING WORD

Complete the comparison:

OIL is to NATURAL GAS as WIND is to ...

A. Sun
B. Coal
C. Nuclear
D. Turbine
E. Renewable

ANSWER:

Puzzle 1.33	**Difficulty rating: 1**

BACKWARDS

If written backwards, would the number, "Three hundred and fifty-one thousand, seven hundred and eighty-six", be written as "six hundred and eighty-seven thousand, one hundred and fifty-three"?

ANSWER:

Puzzle 1.34	Difficulty rating: 1

COMPLETE THE SEQUENCE

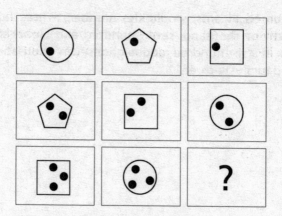

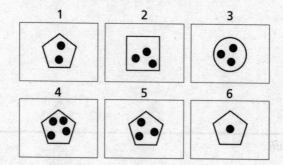

Which one is correct?

ANSWER:

| Puzzle 1.35 | Difficulty rating: 1 |

COOKIES

A new brand of oatmeal cookies are 90 per cent fat-free. How many of the 90 per cent fat-free cookies would I have to eat to ingest the same amount of fat that would be in one regular oatmeal cookie?

ANSWER:

| Puzzle 1.36 | Difficulty rating: 1 |

MISSING WORD

Complete the comparison:

DECOMPRESSION SICKNESS is to THE BENDS as PNEUMOCONIOSIS is to . . .

A. Athlete's Foot
B. Morning sickness
C. Black Lung
D. Lung Water
E. Asthma

ANSWER:

| Puzzle 1.37 | Difficulty rating: 1 |

COMPLETE THE SEQUENCE

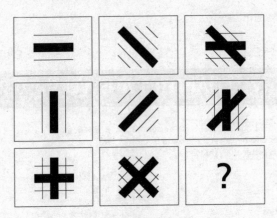

Which one is correct?

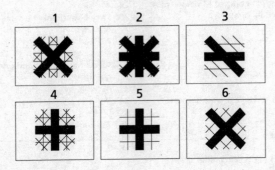

ANSWER:

| Puzzle 1.38 | Difficulty rating: 1 |

39

CHAPTER 1 ANSWERS

1.1 Peter wins again. Peter is the faster runner and he can run the extra 5 meters faster than Duncan.

1.2 C. Grape

1.3 3

1.4 20¢

1.5 B

1.6 B. Africa

1.7 3

1.8 27 rungs (13 above, 13 below, plus the middle one).

1.9 2

1.10 7

1.11 3

1.12 A. Sun

1.13 No

1.14 4

1.15 Josh is the tallest, then Duncan, then Mick.

1.16 B. Brass

1.17 A. True

1.18 5

1.19 Kelly is eight years older than Danielle.

1.20 B. Rhodesia

1.21 No

1.22 21

1.23 3

1.24 Paul is sleeping between Andy and Josh.

1.25 B. Food

1.26 4 (It is the only form with 6 cubes)

1.27 D. Recipe

1.28 4

1.29 They both drank the same amount of caffeine.

1.30 A. Read

1.31 4

1.32 Alison has one cat and one goldfish.

1.33 A. Sun

1.34 Yes

1.35 5

1.36 Ten cookies

1.37 C. Black Lung

1.38 2

DIFFICULTY RATING: 40

FLAGPOLES

There are two flagpoles on the military base. One pole is 16 feet tall and casts a shadow four feet long on the ground. The second flagpole is 64 feet tall. How long would the shadow on the second flagpole be?

ANSWER:

| Puzzle 2.1 | Difficulty rating: 1 |

MISSING WORD

Complete the comparison:

ENGINE is to CYLINDER as BOOK is to . . .

A. Piston
B. Library
C. Shelf
D. Car
E. Pages

ANSWER:

Puzzle 2.2	Difficulty rating: 1

COMPLETE THE SEQUENCE

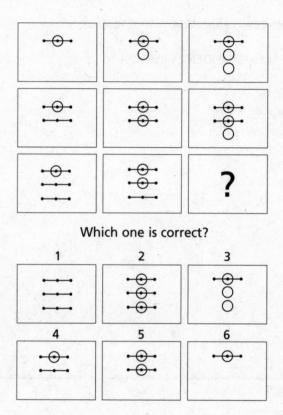

Which one is correct?

ANSWER:

Puzzle 2.3 | Difficulty rating: 1

What is the only U.S. state with one syllable?

ANSWER:

| **Puzzle 2.4** | **Difficulty rating: 1** |

MISSING WORD

Complete the comparison:

ROBBERY is to INCARCERATION as SMOKING is to . . .

A. Cigarettes
B. Lung cancer
C. Prison
D. Matches
E. Tobacco

ANSWER:

COMPLETE THE SEQUENCE

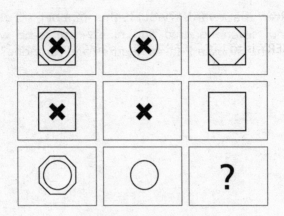

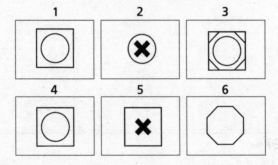

Which one is correct?

ANSWER:

| Puzzle 2.6 | Difficulty rating: 1 |

BACKWARDS

If written backwards, would the number, "Fourteen thousand, seven hundred and ninety-eight", be written, "Eighty-nine thousand, seven hundred and forty-one?"

ANSWER:

| Puzzle 2.7 | Difficulty rating: 1 |

WHICH DAY?

If today is Thursday, what is the day that follows the day that comes after the day that precedes the day before yesterday?

ANSWER:

Puzzle 2.8	Difficulty rating: 1

MISSING WORD

Complete the comparison:

LIGHT BULB is to FILAMENT as WHEEL is to . . .

A. Electricity
B. Road
C. Spoke
D. Automobile
E. Pulley

ANSWER:

Puzzle 2.9	Difficulty rating: 1

COMPLETE THE SEQUENCE

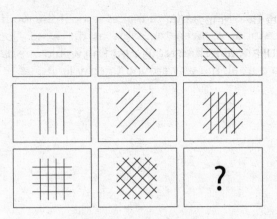

Which one is correct?

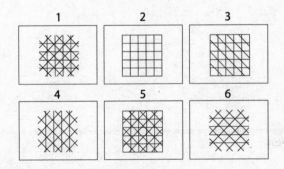

| Puzzle 2.10 | Difficulty rating: 1 |

WORD PUZZLE

Does the following sentence makes sense if the word "puff" is understood to mean the same as the word "jog". The puffers all thought that regular puffing would one day allow them to puff all the way around the city limits.

ANSWER:

Puzzle 2.11	Difficulty rating: 1

GARAGE SALE

Mary Ellen was having a garage sale and someone came by and bought the lawnmower. The person paid $100 for it and paid with a check. Before leaving, he decided he didn't want the lawnmower and wanted the $75 chainsaw instead. Mary Ellen gave the person $25 change and he left. The check later bounced, and she was charged a $25 fee by the bank. If the chainsaw originally cost her $50, how much did she lose?

ANSWER:

| Puzzle 2.12 | Difficulty rating: 1 |

Do the vowels in the word UNCONTROVERSIAL appear in reverse alphabetical order?

ANSWER:

| Puzzle 2.13 | Difficulty rating: 1 |

COMPLETE THE SEQUENCE

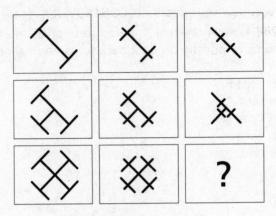

Which one is correct?

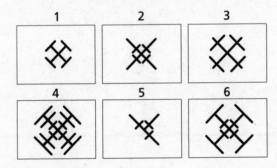

ANSWER:

| Puzzle 2.14 | Difficulty rating: 1 |

PRICE MATCH

A store reduced the price of one of its products by 25 per cent. What percentage of the reduced price must it be increased by to put the product back to its original price?

A. 25 per cent
B. 30 per cent
C. 33.3333 per cent
D. 50 per cent
E. 66 per cent

ANSWER:

| Puzzle 2.15 | Difficulty rating: 1 |

MISSING WORD

Complete the comparison:

WALES is to UK as POLAND is to . . .

A. Ukraine
B. USSR
C. EU
D. Euro
E. Warsaw Pact

ANSWER:

| Puzzle 2.16 | Difficulty rating: 1 |

WORD PUZZLE

Do the words, RESERVE, SERVERS, and VERSES all use the exact same letters?

ANSWER:

| Puzzle 2.17 | Difficulty rating: 1 |

COMPLETE THE SEQUENCE

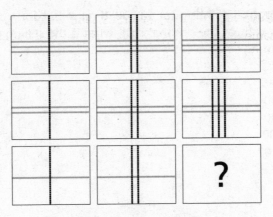

Which one is correct?

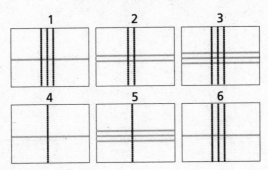

ANSWER:

| Puzzle 2.18 | Difficulty rating: 1 |

ART COLLECTOR

Josh bought a painting for $8,000. If he sells it for a profit of 12.5 per cent of the original cost, what is the selling price of the painting?

A. $8,125
B. $8,800
C. $9,000
D. $9,500
E. $10,000

ANSWER:

| Puzzle 2.19 | Difficulty rating: 1 |

MISSING WORD

BISHOP is to CHESS as SOLDIER is to . . .

A. Commander
B. Battle map
C. Government
D. Gun
E. War

ANSWER:

| Puzzle 2.20 | Difficulty rating: 1 |

VOWELS

Is the thirteenth vowel appearing in this sentence the letter "e"?

ANSWER:

COMPLETE THE SEQUENCE

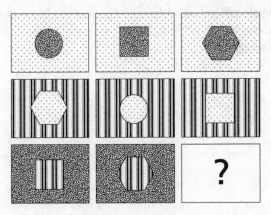

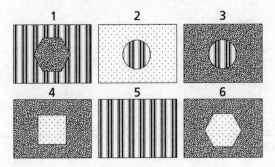

Which one is correct?

1   2   3

4   5   6

ANSWER:

Puzzle 2.22	Difficulty rating: 1

SHIP AT SEA

A ship floats with three-fifths of its weight above the water. What is the ratio of the ship's submerged weight to its exposed weight?

A. 3 : 8
B. 2 : 5
C. 3 : 5
D. 2 : 3
E. 5 : 3

ANSWER:

Puzzle 2.23	Difficulty rating: 1

MISSING WORD

Complete the comparison:

BOOK is to LIBRARY as PAINTING is to . . .

A. Artists
B. Building
C. Curator
D. Easel
E. Gallery

ANSWER:

Puzzle 2.24	Difficulty rating: 1

COMPLETE THE SEQUENCE

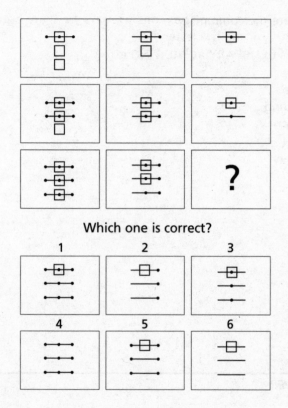

Which one is correct?

ANSWER:

Puzzle 2.25 | Difficulty rating: 2

ALPHABET

In the English alphabet, how many letters are there between the letter "o" and the letter "v"?

ANSWER:

| Puzzle 2.26 | Difficulty rating: 1 |

EARNINGS

Dan's weekly salary is $70 less than Jerry's, whose weekly salary is $50 more than Sally's. If Sally earns $280 per week, how much does Dan earn per week?

ANSWER:

| Puzzle 2.27 | Difficulty rating: 1 |

MISSING WORD

Complete the comparison:

FIRE is to SMOKE as POLLUTION is to . . .

A. Damage
B. Garbage
C. Acid rain
D. Resources
E. Environment

ANSWER:

| Puzzle 2.28 | Difficulty rating: 1 |

WORD PUZZLE

If the word PAIN is written under the word STAR and the word PACE is written under the word PAIN and the word LICK is written under the word PACE, is then the word SACK formed diagonally?

ANSWER:

BOOK PRICE

A certain book costs $12 more in hardcover than in softcover. If the softcover price is two-thirds of the hardcover price, how much does the book cost in hardcover?

ANSWER:

Puzzle 2.30	Difficulty rating: 1

MISSING WORD

Complete the comparison:

GAUDY is to OSTENTATIOUS as POVERTY is to . . .

A. Misery
B. Penury
C. Poorhouse
D. Hunger

ANSWER:

| Puzzle 2.31 | Difficulty rating: 1 |

If you remove ten letters from the word INTERPLANETARY, can the word RANT be formed?

ANSWER:

| Puzzle 2.32 | Difficulty rating: 1 |

COMPLETE THE SEQUENCE

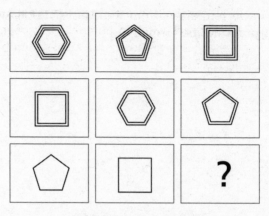

Which one is correct?

1   2   3

4   5   6

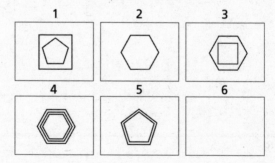

ANSWER:

Puzzle 2.33	Difficulty rating: 1

GUMBALLS

There are enough gumballs in a bag to give 12 gumballs to each of the 20 children, with no gumballs left over. If five children do not want any gumballs, how many gumballs can be given to each of the others?

ANSWER:

Puzzle 2.34	Difficulty rating: 1

MISSING WORD

Complete the comparison:

REMUNERATIVE is to PROFITABLE as PLOT is to . . .

A. Conspire
B. Entice
C. Deduce
D. Respire

ANSWER:

Puzzle 2.35	Difficulty rating: 1

Is the following sentence spelled the same forwards as it is backwards?

BUST TO HOT STUB

ANSWER:

| Puzzle 2.36 | Difficulty rating: 1 |

SUBWAY

A subway car passes an average of three stations every ten minutes. At this rate, how many stations will it pass in one hour?

ANSWER:

| Puzzle 2.37 | Difficulty rating: 1 |

COMPLETE THE SEQUENCE

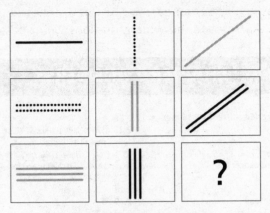

Which one is correct?

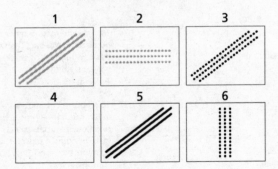

ANSWER:

| Puzzle 2.38 | Difficulty rating: 1 |

CHAPTER 2 ANSWERS

2.1 16 feet. (64 ÷ 16) x 4 = 16 feet
2.2 E. Pages
2.3 2
2.4 Maine.
2.5 B. Lung cancer
2.6 6
2.7 Yes
2.8 Wednesday
2.9 C. Spoke
2.10 1
2.11 Yes
2.12 She lost $100.
2.13 No
2.14 2
2.15 C. 33.3333 per cent
2.16 C. EU
2.17 No
2.18 6
2.19 C. $9,000
2.20 E. War
2.21 No
2.22 3
2.23 D. 2 : 3
2.24 E. Gallery
2.25 3

2.26 6
2.27 $260. Sally makes $280. If Jerry makes $50 more than this, then Jerry must make $280 + $50 or $330. Dan makes $70 less than this amount, or $260.
2.28 C. Acid rain
2.29 Yes
2.30 $36
2.31 B. Penury
2.32 Yes
2.33 2
2.34 16. Find the total number of gumballs in the bag, then divide by the new number of children who will be sharing them.
2.35 A. Conspire
2.36 No
2.37 18 stations. The subway will pass 60 ÷ 10 or 6 times as many stations in one hour as it passes in 10 minutes. In 10 minutes it passes 3 stations; in 60 minutes it must pass 6 x 3, or 18 stations.
2.38 3

DIFFICULTY RATING: 54

TICK TOCK

How many times does the minute hand pass the hour hand between noon and midnight on a normal clock?

ANSWER:

WHO WINS?

Which of the following numbers does not fit in with the pattern of the series?

64 54 42 31 20

ANSWER:

| Puzzle 3.2 | Difficulty rating: 2 |

Complete the comparison:

FAITH is to PRAYER as WORK is to . . .

A. Entertainment
B. Church
C. Income
D. Office

ANSWER:

| Puzzle 3.3 | Difficulty rating: 1 |

MARATHON

Jess is planning on running the Boston marathon and the New York City marathon. Jess finds a store that has sneakers on sale and she wants to buy enough sneakers to get through both marathons. If each marathon is 26 miles and each pair of sneakers lasts ten miles, how many pairs of sneakers should Jess buy?

ANSWER:

| Puzzle 3.4 | Difficulty rating: 2 |

COMPLETE THE SEQUENCE

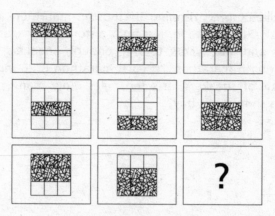

Which one is correct?

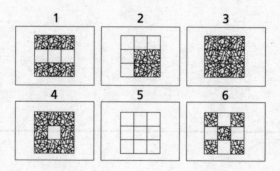

ANSWER:

| Puzzle 3.5 | Difficulty rating: 1 |

MISSING WORD

Complete the comparison:

CHAFF is to WHEAT as DREGS is to . . .

A. Society
B. Wine
C. Denizens
D. Stalk

ANSWER:

Puzzle 3.6	Difficulty rating: 1

RAINY DAYS

Patti moved to Seattle and wasn't used to all the rain. She decided to make a rain gauge to measure the amount of rain for one week. It rained each day that week, starting on Monday, and each day the amount of rain in the gauge doubled. By the following Sunday, the rain gauge was completely filled. On which day was the rain gauge half-filled?

ANSWER:

| Puzzle 3.7 | Difficulty rating: 2 |

WARM UP

Jess decides to run 20 miles to warm up for the marathon. She ran the first half at five miles per hour and ran the second half at ten miles per hour. What was her average speed?

ANSWER:

Puzzle 3.8	Difficulty rating: 2

WORD PUZZLE

Do the words DECLINES, LICENSED, and SILENCED all use the exact same letters?

ANSWER:

Puzzle 3.9	Difficulty rating: 1

COMPLETE THE SEQUENCE

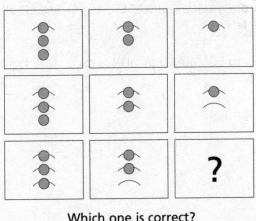

Which one is correct?

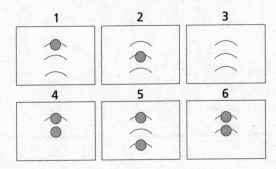

ANSWER:

| Puzzle 3.10 | Difficulty rating: 1 |

MISSING WORD

Complete the comparison:

HOLSTER is to SCABBARD as GUN is to . . .

A. Beatle
B. Sword
C. Bullet
D. Armory

ANSWER:

| Puzzle 3.11 | Difficulty rating: 1 |

BATTING BALLS

During spring training Derek and Bernie were practicing hitting balls. On Derek's first time at bat, he hit 75 out of 100 pitches. Then Bernie hit 75 out of 100 pitches. On Derek's second turn at bat he hit 35 of the 50 pitches thrown. Bernie didn't take a second turn at bat. Who had the best average for the day – Derek or Bernie?

ANSWER:

COMPLETE THE SEQUENCE

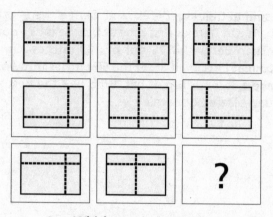

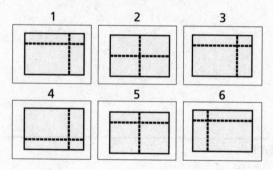

Which one is correct?

ANSWER:

Puzzle 3.13   Difficulty rating: 1

94

WORD PUZZLE

BEGIN and BEGUN are:

A. Similar
B. Dissimilar
C. Opposite

ANSWER:

| **Puzzle 3.14** | **Difficulty rating: 1** |

MISSING WORD

Complete the comparison:

GRAPE is to APPLE as VINE is to . . .

A. Juice
B. Yard
C. Pear
D. Tree

ANSWER:

| Puzzle 3.15 | Difficulty rating: 1 |

AIRPORT CLOCKS

At LaGuardia airport there are three clocks in the terminal. Clock A says it's 8:00, clock B says it's 8:50 and clock C says it's 8:20. One of the clocks is 20 minutes fast, one is slow, and one is off by half an hour. What is the actual time?

ANSWER:

| Puzzle 3.16 | Difficulty rating: 2 |

COMPLETE THE SEQUENCE

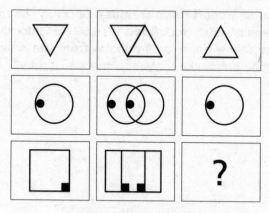

Which one is correct?

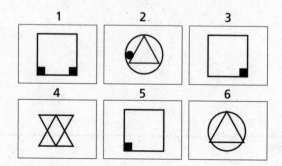

ANSWER:

| Puzzle 3.17 | Difficulty rating: 1 |

GOLD RINGS

A jeweler is producing gold rings. For every 11 rings he makes, he has enough scrap gold to be melted into one extra ring. How many rings can he make from the scrap after making 250 gold rings?

ANSWER:

| Puzzle 3.18 | Difficulty rating: 2 |

MISSING WORD

Complete the comparison:

INDIA is to PAKISTAN as SPAIN is to . . .

A. Cambodia
B. Portugal
C. Balearic Islands
D. Mexico

ANSWER:

| Puzzle 3.19 | Difficulty rating: 1 |

COMPLETE THE SEQUENCE

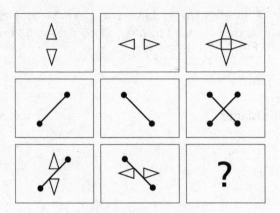

Which one is correct?

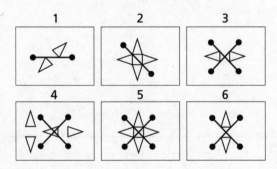

ANSWER:

COOKIES

It takes 17 minutes for 17 bakers to bake 17 cookies. How many bakers do you need to bake 51 cookies in 51 minutes?

ANSWER:

Puzzle 3.21	Difficulty rating: 2

COMPLETE THE SEQUENCE

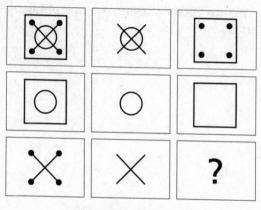

Which one is correct?

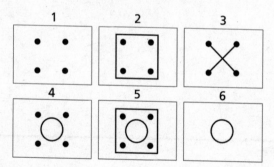

ANSWER:

| Puzzle 3.22 | Difficulty rating: 1 |

VOWELS

Is "o" the seventh vowel of this particular phrase?

ANSWER:

MISSING WORD

Complete the comparison:

JUNE is to MARCH as DECEMBER is to . . .

A. September
B. August
C. July
D. January

ANSWER:

Puzzle 3.24	Difficulty rating: 1

CATS

The cat named Coco is heavier than the cat named Lulu. Winston weighs more than Fluffy but less than Rocky. Fluffy weighs more than Lulu. Rocky weighs less than Coco. List the cats in the order of their weights, starting with the heaviest.

ANSWER:

Puzzle 3.25	Difficulty rating: 2

COMPLETE THE SEQUENCE

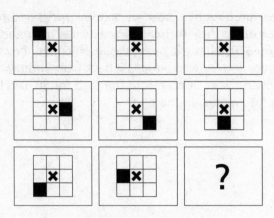

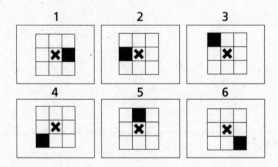

Which one is correct?

ANSWER:

| Puzzle 3.26 | Difficulty rating: 1 |

BASEBALL CARDS

Little Duncan bought a pack of baseball cards and found a rookie card worth $10. He decided to sell it to his friend Tommy for $10. After the baseball season ended the card was worth more and Duncan bought it back from Tommy for $15. The following year Duncan sold the card for $8. Did Duncan make or lose money in the end?

ANSWER:

Puzzle 3.27	Difficulty rating: 2

MISSING WORD

Complete the comparison:

RAISIN is to PRUNE as GRAPE is to . . .

A. Vine
B. Berry
C. Plum
D. Seed

ANSWER:

| **Puzzle 3.28** | **Difficulty rating: 1** |

COMPLETE THE SEQUENCE

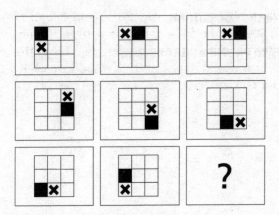

Which one is correct?

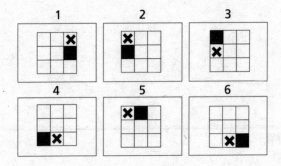

ANSWER:

| Puzzle 3.29 | Difficulty rating: 1 |

110

FINDERS KEEPERS

Jackie was walking down the street and found $4 on the sidewalk. She put the $4 in her purse with the money she had before she found it and she now had five times the amount of money she would have had if she had lost $4. How much money did Jackie have before she found the $4?

ANSWER:

| Puzzle 3.30 | Difficulty rating: 2 |

SHOE CRAZE

Patricia loves her shoes. She has ten pairs of shoes in five different colors. Patricia is a particularly lazy person though, and just tosses her shoes in a bin when she takes them off. She needs to go away for a weekend on business but she put off packing until really early in the morning. It's still dark outside and she can't see the colors in the bins. How many individual shoes will she have to take out of the bin to be sure that she has at least two of the same color?

ANSWER:

| Puzzle 3.31 | Difficulty rating: 2 |

WORD PUZZLE

If you remove seven letters from the word WINDSURFING, can the word GRIND be formed?

ANSWER:

| **Puzzle 3.32** | **Difficulty rating: 1** |

MISSING WORD

Complete the comparison:

SUMMER is to WINTER as NEW YORK is to . . .

A. Fall
B. Sydney
C. London
D. Rain

ANSWER:

| Puzzle 3.33 | Difficulty rating: 1 |

SNAIL PACE

A snail is at the bottom of a ten-foot well. He climbs three feet a day, but during the night, while resting, he slips back two feet. At this rate, how many days will it take the snail to climb out of the well?

ANSWER:

COMPLETE THE SEQUENCE

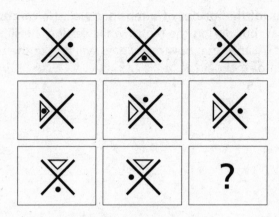

Which one is correct?

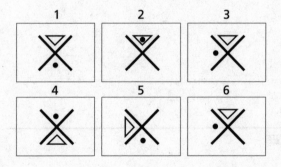

ANSWER:

| Puzzle 3.35 | Difficulty rating: 1 |

Which one of the following numbers doesn't fit the pattern?

5/8 9/24 1/4 2/16 0

ANSWER:

Puzzle 3.36	Difficulty rating: 2

MISSING WORD

Complete the comparison:

STREAM is to RIVER as POND is to . . .

A. Brook
B. Fish
C. Water
D. Lake

ANSWER:

| Puzzle 3.37 | Difficulty rating: 1 |

FLIES AND SPIDERS

If you have a group of six-legged flies and eight-legged spiders and there are 48 legs in total, how many flies and how many spiders are there in the group?

ANSWER:

CHAPTER 3 ANSWERS

3.1 It only passes ten times.
3.2 54. The interval between each number is 11.
3.3 C. Income
3.4 Six pairs. Five pairs will only get her 50 miles and both marathons are 52 miles.
3.5 3
3.6 B. Wine
3.7 The rain gauge was half-filled on Saturday. It doubled on Sunday, to become completely filled.
3.8 It takes Jess two hours to run the first 10 miles and one hour to run the last 10 miles, meaning she needs three hours to run the total of 20 miles. Therefore, her average speed is 6.7 miles per hour.

3.9 Yes
3.10 1
3.11 B. Sword
3.12 Bernie had the best average. Derek batted 73 per cent and Bernie an average of 75 per cent.
3.13 6
3.14 A. Similar
3.15 D. Tree
3.16 The time is 8:30.
3.17 5
3.18 22 additional gold rings. 11 rings produce 12, and as no scrap is derived from each 12th ring then "11" produces 12 every time, so "110" produces 120, "220" produces 240, "231" produces 252, "242" produces 264 – a surplus of

22. After making 242 rings, only 8 more rings are required to bring the production up to 250 rings, and 8 rings produce insufficient scrap to make an extra ring. So the surplus produced remains at 22 (or 22.73, strictly speaking).

3.19 B. Portugal

3.20 5

3.21 You still only need 17 bakers.

3.22 1

3.23 No, it is an "e".

3.24 A. September

3.25 Coco, Rocky, Winston, Fluffy, and Lulu.

3.26 3

3.27 Duncan sold the card twice, for $10 and $8. He paid $15 for the card so he came out ahead by $3.

3.28 C. Plum

3.29 3

3.30 Jackie had $6 before she found the $4.

3.31 Six shoes. If she takes out five shoes, she could have one of each color, with no two matching colors.

3.32 No

3.33 B. Sydney

3.34 Eight days. The snail makes one foot of progress every 24 hours. So after seven days, he will have climbed seven feet. Then on day eight, he will climb the three feet he manages per day and gets out of the well.

3.35 2

3.36 $\frac{5}{8}$. Subtract 0.125 from each until you reach zero.

3.37 D. Lake

3.38 Four flies (24 legs) and three spiders (24 legs). No other combination will work.

DIFFICULTY RATING: 58

TUG OF WAR

Two rival colleges decided to a tug of war. From their starting positions college A pulls College B forward 3 meters, and are then pulled forward themselves 5 meters. College B then pulls College A forward 2 meters. If the first college to be pulled forward 10 meters loses, how many more meters must college B pull College A forward to win?

ANSWER:

| Puzzle 4.1 | Difficulty rating: 1 |

NUMBER SEQUENCE

Pick the number that follows the pattern set by the series:

0 1 3 6 10 . . .

ANSWER:

MISSING WORD

Complete the comparison:

BLANCHED is to PALLID as REGALE is to . . .

A. Entertain
B. Remain
C. Contorted
D. Baked

ANSWER:

| Puzzle 4.3 | Difficulty rating: 1 |

COMPLETE THE SEQUENCE

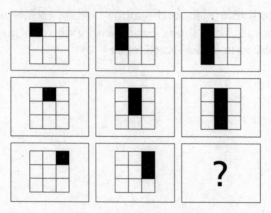

Which one is correct?

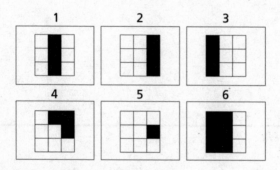

ANSWER:

| Puzzle 4.4 | Difficulty rating: 1 |

127

HANDSHAKES

There were four men in the lobby waiting to interview for the same job. They shook hands with each other just once. How many handshakes were made?

ANSWER:

| Puzzle 4.5 | Difficulty rating: 2 |

MISSING WORD

Complete the comparison:

PLETHORA is to DEARTH as SCARCE is to . . .

A. Abundant
B. Few
C. Cornucopia
D. Hardly

ANSWER:

| Puzzle 4.6 | Difficulty rating: 1 |

CIDS AND BOFS

Rars are three times as long as Bofs. Cids are three times as long as Rars. That means:

A. Cids are six times as long as Bofs.
B. Bofs are six times as long as Cids.
C. Cids are nine times as long as Bofs.
D. Bofs are nine times as long as Cids.

ANSWER:

| Puzzle 4.7 | Difficulty rating: 2 |

COMPLETE THE SEQUENCE

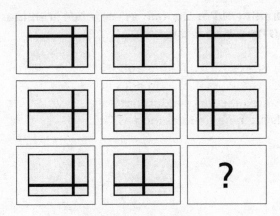

Which one is correct?

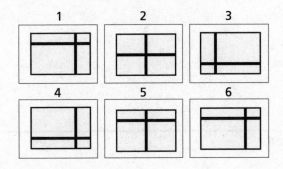

ANSWER:

| Puzzle 4.8 | Difficulty rating: 1 |

131

WHO IS OLDER?

If Lauren is as old as Duncan will be when Trish is as old as Lauren is now, who is the oldest?

ANSWER:

MEXICAN

Josh went to Mexico and bought a painting for $2,500. When he came home his friend Lance saw the painting and gave Josh $3,500 for it. A few days later, Josh bought the painting back for $4,500, thinking it would be worth more some day. He took it to an art dealer who offered him $5,500 for it so Josh sold it to the art dealer. Did Josh make money or lose money in the end?

ANSWER:

Puzzle 4.10	Difficulty rating: 2

FISHING

Tom and Harry caught a dozen fish. Harry caught twice as many as Tom. How many did Tom catch?

ANSWER:

| Puzzle 4.11 | Difficulty rating: 2 |

OUT OF PLACE

While driving the Autobahn Mr. Pickles sees two license plates with interesting configurations. All the letters on both license plates have a logical order, except for one. There is a single letter on the German plate that belongs on the French plate, can you find it?

ANSWER:

COMPLETE THE SEQUENCE

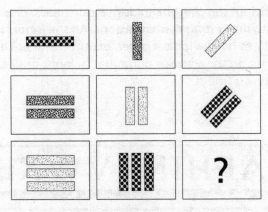

Which one is correct?

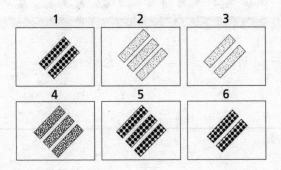

MARBLE SHARE

Steve and Lisa each have a bag containing the same number of marbles. How many marbles must Steve give Lisa so Lisa will have ten more marbles than Steve?

ANSWER:

| Puzzle 4.14 | Difficulty rating: 2 |

NAMES PUZZLE

John
Ogden
——→ ?

Adam
Joseph
——→ SMITH

Ian
Alexander
——→ FLEMING

ANSWER:

| Puzzle 4.15 | Difficulty rating: 1 |

LETTER SEQUENCE

Which letter does not belong in the sequence?

C F J M Q U

ANSWER:

BLOCKS

Using only the small gray block, can you make an exact replica of the large L-shaped block using a number of the small L-shaped blocks? Rotating and reflecting the gray block are allowed.

ANSWER:

| Puzzle 4.17 | Difficulty rating: 2 |

COMPLETE THE SEQUENCE

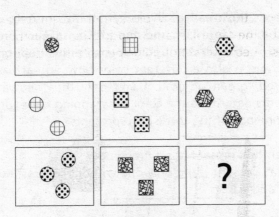

Which one is correct?

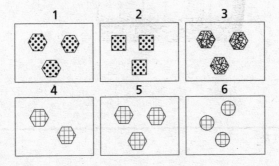

ANSWER:

| Puzzle 4.18 | Difficulty rating: 1 |

141

CHRISTMAS

Under the Christmas tree there were three presents, one for Samantha, one for Mary, and one for Louisa. Each present is wrapped with a different color paper, either red, green or silver. There is also a different color bow on each present, either red, green or gold. Using only the following two statements determine the color of wrapping paper and bow that is on each of the three girls' presents.

1. Samantha's present has a green bow.
2. Louisa's present is the only one without contrasting colors of bow and paper.

ANSWER:

| Puzzle 4.19 | Difficulty rating: 2 |

MISSING WORD

Complete the comparison:

COSTLY is to CHEAP as RESCIND is to . . .

A. Refuse
B. Validate
C. Parsimonious
D. Rest

ANSWER:

Puzzle 4.20	Difficulty rating: 1

COMPLETE THE SEQUENCE

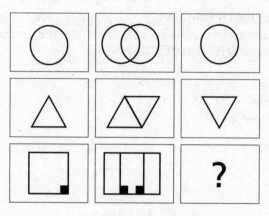

Which one is correct?

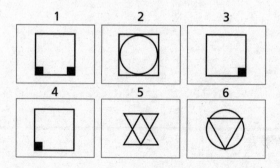

ANSWER:

| Puzzle 4.21 | Difficulty rating: 1 |

BACKWARDS

If written backwards, would the number, "two thousand, four hundred and sixty nine", be written, "nine thousand, six hundred and forty-two"?

ANSWER:

| Puzzle 4.22 | Difficulty rating: 1 |

TOURNAMENT

A single-elimination billiards tournament is held for 100 players. How many matches will be played before a winner is crowned?

ANSWER:

PUZZLE PIECE

Pick the piece that is missing from the puzzle.

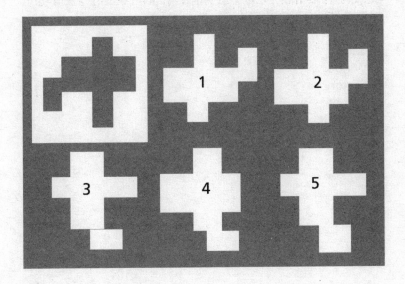

ANSWER:

Puzzle 4.24	Difficulty rating: 2

MISSING WORD

Complete the comparison:

PAPER is to TREE as GLASS is to . . .

A. Sand
B. Window
C. Factory
D. Lumber
E. Element

ANSWER:

| Puzzle 4.25 | Difficulty rating: 1 |

ZOO COUNT

A zoo has some lions and some ostriches. The zoo keeper counted 15 heads and 50 legs. How many lions were there?

ANSWER:

| Puzzle 4.26 | Difficulty rating: 2 |

BRONGS AND GROLS

If most Reebings are Brongs and some Reebings are Grols, the statement that some Brongs are Grols is:

A. True
B. False
C. Indeterminable from data

ANSWER:

| Puzzle 4.27 | Difficulty rating: 2 |

MISSING WORD

Complete the comparison:

LEONARDO DA VINCI is to RENAISSANCE as VOLTAIRE is to . . .

A. Existentialism
B. Reformation
C. Romanticism
D. Enlightenment
E. Post Modernism

ANSWER:

| Puzzle 4.28 | Difficulty rating: 1 |

COMPLETE THE SEQUENCE

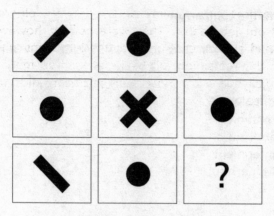

Which one is correct?

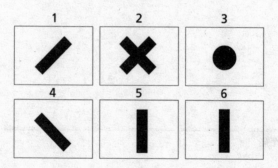

ANSWER:

Puzzle 4.29	Difficulty rating: 1

OFFICE PARTY

At the office party Tommy and Ally were planning on handing out jellybeans. They were hungry, however, and Tommy had already eaten half of the jellybeans when Ally ate half the remaining jellybeans plus three more. There were no jellybeans left. How many jellybeans did they take to the office party?

ANSWER:

Puzzle 4.30	Difficulty rating: 2

MISSING WORD

Complete the comparison:

SKINNER is to FREUD as BEHAVIORISM is to . . .

A. Naturalism
B. Skinner Box
C. Psychoanalysis
D. Socialism
E. Psychology

ANSWER:

| Puzzle 4.31 | Difficulty rating: 1 |

FAKE COIN

A man was given eight silver dollar coins. However, one of them was fake and he did not know if the fake coin weighed more or less than the other coins. What is the minimum number of weighings that it would take to guarantee him finding the counterfeit coin? Assume a balance scale is used.

ANSWER:

| Puzzle 4.32 | Difficulty rating: 2 |

COMPLETE THE SEQUENCE

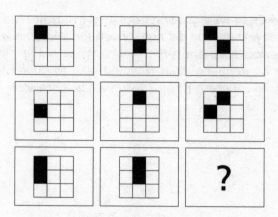

Which one is correct?

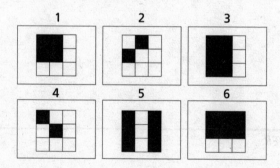

Puzzle 4.33	Difficulty rating: 1

POOL GAME

Dan and Craig were playing pool for $1 a game. At the end of the day, Dan won $4 and Craig won three times. How many games did they play?

ANSWER:

MISSING WORD

Complete the comparison:

KEYNES is to DARWIN as ECONOMICS is to . . .

A. Naturalist
B. Creationism
C. Mathematics
D. Colonialism
E. Evolution

ANSWER:

| Puzzle 4.35 | Difficulty rating: 1 |

TEASER

Is it possible for Peggy to have seven children if half of them are girls?

ANSWER:

COMPLETE THE SEQUENCE

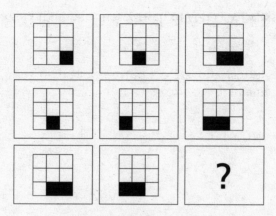

Which one is correct?

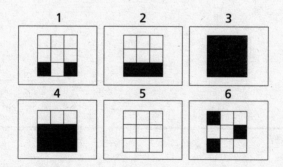

ANSWER:

| Puzzle 4.37 | Difficulty rating: 1 |

WORD PLAY

T A E F N U L N E W T O T R E D R S

Using the letters above cross out ten letters in such a way that the remaining letters spell a fun word.

ANSWER:

| Puzzle 4.38 | Difficulty rating: 2 |

CHAPTER 4 ANSWERS

4.1   6 meters. Find out how far college A has moved thus far. They pulled college B forward 3 meters, so A moved backward 3 meters. Then they were pulled forward 5 meters and then a further 2 meters. In total then they have moved forward (-3) + 5 + 2 = 4 meters. They must be pulled a further 6 meters to be pulled 10 meters forward.

4.2   15. The interval between each number follows the series 0, 1, 2, 3, 4...

4.3   A. Entertain

4.4   2

4.5   Six handshakes

4.6   A. Abundant

4.7   C. Cids are nine times as long as Bofs

4.8   3

4.9   Lauren

4.10 Josh spent $2,500 and $4,500 for a total of $7,000. Josh sold the painting for $3,500 and $5,500 for a total of $9,000. Josh came out ahead by $2,000.

4.11 4

4.12 Z. Letters on the French plate all have straight lines, while the letters on the German plate do not, except for Z.

4.13 4

4.14 Steve must give Lisa five marbles. He would then have five less, she would have five more for a difference of ten.

4.15 NASH, for John Nash and Ogden Nash

4.16 U. The interval between each letter follows a sequence 2, 3, 2, 3...

4.17

4.18 5

4.19 The only matching colors available for Louisa's present is red paper and a red bow. The only contrasting paper color remaining for Samantha's present is silver. Mary's present is left with green paper and a gold bow.

4.20 B. Validate

4.21 4

4.22 Yes

4.23 99. With only one winner there must be 99 losers, requiring 99 matches.

4.24 3

4.25 A. Sand

4.26 Ten lions

4.27 C. Indeterminable from data

4.28 D. Enlightenment

4.29 1

4.30 12 jellybeans. Ally ate half the remaining jellybeans plus three more to leave none, so she must have eaten six jellybeans. Tommy ate half the jellybeans and left six, meaning there were 12 to start.

4.31 C. Psychoanalysis

4.32 Three weighings. The man has eight coins so he puts two on each side of the scale, if it balances out he puts the four aside since they all weigh the same. Now he knows the lighter/heavier coin is in the remaining four, so he puts these on the scale of the second weighing and whichever side it tilts to, he takes the two coins on that side and reweighs them a third time to find the odd one out.

4.33 1

4.34 Ten games. Craig won the first three, and Dan had to win the next seven in order to win $4 overall.

4.35 E. Evolution

4.36 Yes. She has seven daughters: half of them are girls, and the other half are girls too.

4.37 2

4.38 Cross out every other letter, starting with T. This eliminates TEN LETTERS, leaving A FUN WORD shown:

T A E F N U L N E W T O T R E D R S

5

DIFFICULTY RATING: 60

MISSING WORD

Complete the comparison:

SAND is to PAPYRUS as GLASS is to . . .

A. Reeds
B. Stone
C. Paper
D. Egyptian

ANSWER:

Puzzle 5.1	Difficulty rating: 1

CARPETS

It takes Mary one hour to install carpet on a bedroom floor that is 9 feet wide and 12 feet long. How long will it take her to put carpet on the living room floor, which is twice as wide and twice as long?

ANSWER:

CAR SALE

A car dealer spent $20,000 buying some used cars. He sold them for $27,500 making an average of $1,500 on each car. How many cars did he sell?

ANSWER:

Puzzle 5.3	Difficulty rating: 2

COMPLETE THE SEQUENCE

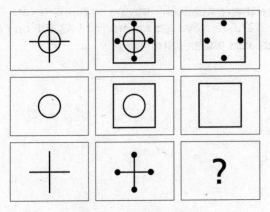

Which one is correct?

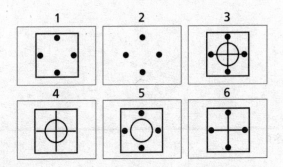

ANSWER:

| Puzzle 5.4 | Difficulty rating: 1 |

MISSING WORD

Complete the comparison:

BUILDING is to RAZE as SHIP is to . . .

A. Sail
B. Scuttle
C. Dock
D. Moor

ANSWER:

Puzzle 5.5	**Difficulty rating: 1**

WIRE CUTTING

You have a spool with 100 meters of wire. You need 100 lengths of wire that are one meter long each. If it takes you one second to measure and cut each meter, how long will it take you to come up with 100 pieces of wire?

ANSWER:

| Puzzle 5.6 | Difficulty rating: 2 |

MISSING WORD

Complete the comparison:

WHEEL is to SPOKE as FORK is to . . .

A. Handle
B. Tine
C. Road
D. Plate

ANSWER:

| Puzzle 5.7 | Difficulty rating: 1 |

COMPLETE THE SEQUENCE

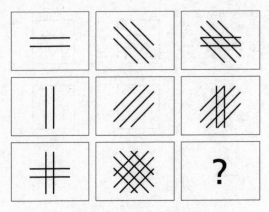

Which one is correct?

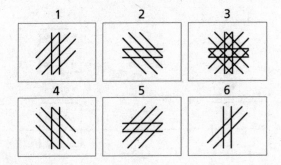

ANSWER:

| Puzzle 5.8 | Difficulty rating: 1 |

COMPLETE THE SEQUENCE

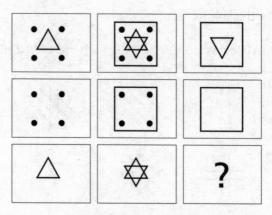

Which one is correct?

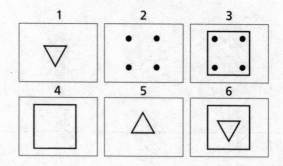

ANSWER:

| Puzzle 5.9 | Difficulty rating: 1 |

MISSING WORD

Complete the comparison:

MOAI STATUES is to EASTER ISLAND as STONEHENGE is to . . .

A. Ireland
B. England
C. Scotland
D. Wales

ANSWER:

| Puzzle 5.10 | Difficulty rating: 1 |

COMPLETE THE SEQUENCE

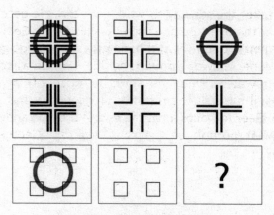

Which one is correct?

| Puzzle 5.11 | Difficulty rating: 1 |

SUBWAY SLEEP

George takes the subway to work each day. He gets on the subway at the first stop and usually takes a nap. George falls asleep when the subway still has twice as far to go as it has already gone. Midway through the ride, George wakes up to check his watch. When he starts to doze off again the subway still has half the distance to go that it has already traveled. George wakes up at the end of the ride and goes to work. What portion of the total ride did George sleep through?

ANSWER:

| Puzzle 5.12 | Difficulty rating: 2 |

MISSING WORD

Complete the comparison:

. . . is to BRAZIL as POUND is to UNITED KINGDOM

A. Yuan
B. Bhat
C. Real
D. Peso
E. Euro

ANSWER:

Puzzle 5.13	Difficulty rating: 2

COMPLETE THE SEQUENCE

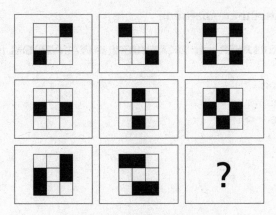

Which one is correct?

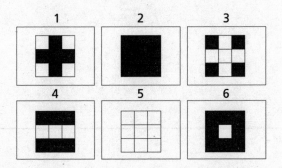

ANSWER:

Puzzle 5.14	Difficulty rating: 1

MISSING WORD

Complete the comparison:

LEXICOGRAPHER is to DICTIONARY as WAINWRIGHT is to . . .

A. Wagon
B. Screenplay
C. Schooner
D. Law

ANSWER:

Puzzle 5.15	Difficulty rating: 1

COMPLETE THE SEQUENCE

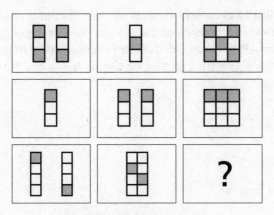

Which one is correct?

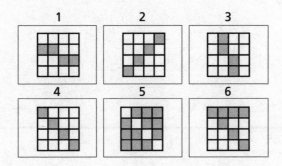

ANSWER:

| Puzzle 5.16 | Difficulty rating: 2 |

BIRTHDAY CAKE

Mary Ellen has seven people at her birthday party and everyone wants a piece of cake. How can Mary Ellen cut the cake into eight pieces if she's only allowed to make three straight cuts and she can't move the pieces as she cuts them?

ANSWER:

Puzzle 5.17	Difficulty rating: 2

MISSING WORD

Complete the comparison:

LIQUOR is to ALCOHOLISM as FOOD is to . . .

A. Overindulgence
B. Obesity
C. Calories
D. Candy
E. Stomach

ANSWER:

Puzzle 5.18	Difficulty rating: 2

COMPLETE THE SEQUENCE

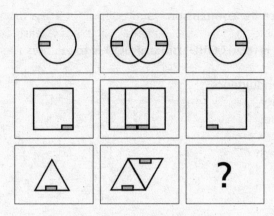

Which one is correct?

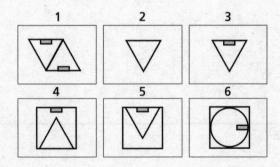

| **Puzzle 5.19** | **Difficulty rating: 1** |

MISSING WORD

Complete the comparison:

DISCOMFORT is to PAIN as UPRISING is to . . .

A. Anesthesia
B. Marxist
C. Revolution
D. Settlement

ANSWER:

| **Puzzle 5.20** | **Difficulty rating: 1** |

COMPLETE THE SEQUENCE

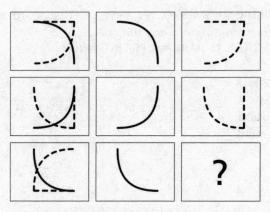

Which one is correct?

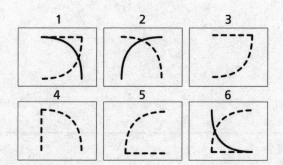

| Puzzle 5.21 | Difficulty rating: 1 |

TIC TAC TOE

Is it possible to put six Xs on a Tic Tac Toe board without making three-in-a-row in any direction?

ANSWER:

| Puzzle 5.22 | Difficulty rating: 2 |

MISSING WORD

Complete the comparison:

OSS is to CIA as . . . is to UNITED NATIONS

A. Treaty of Versailles
B. League of Nations
C. House of Commons
D. Commonwealth
E. FBI

ANSWER:

| **Puzzle 5.23** | **Difficulty rating: 2** |

COMPLETE THE SEQUENCE

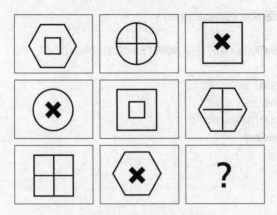

Which one is correct?

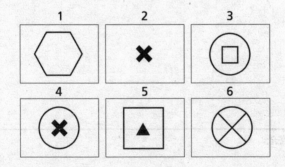

ANSWER:

| Puzzle 5.24 | Difficulty rating: 1 |

MISSING WORD

Complete the comparison:

LANDMARK is to PRESERVING as OPERA HOUSE is to . . .

A. La Scala
B. Singing
C. *La Boheme*
D. Possessing

ANSWER:

COMPLETE THE SEQUENCE

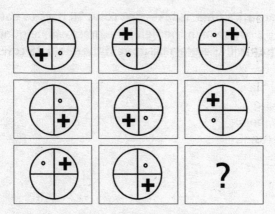

Which one is correct?

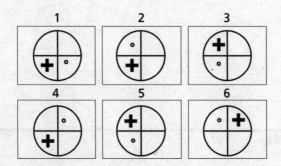

Puzzle 5.26 | **Difficulty rating: 2**

JACK'S COWS

In farmer Jack's field, it takes ten cows 20 days to eat all the grass. If 15 cows are in the field, the grass will be gone in ten days. When will the grass be gone if there are 25 cows in the field?

ANSWER:

Complete the comparison:

MAH JONGG is to GO as TILES is to . . .

A. Pieces
B. Dominoes
C. Cards
D. Grout
E. Stones

ANSWER:

Puzzle 5.28	Difficulty rating: 2

COMPLETE THE SEQUENCE

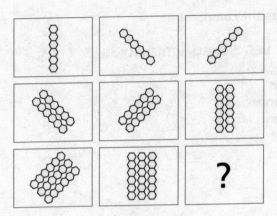

Which one is correct?

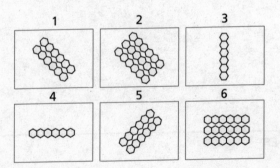

ANSWER:

Puzzle 5.29 | Difficulty rating: 2

MISSING WORD

Complete the comparison:

BOOT is to SANDAL as ARTILLERY SHELL is to . . .

A. Canon
B. Uniform
C. Gunpowder
D. Bullet

ANSWER:

Puzzle 5.30	Difficulty rating: 1

COMPLETE THE SEQUENCE

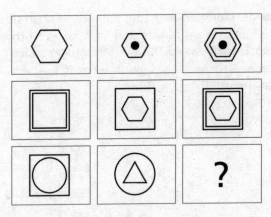

Which one is correct?

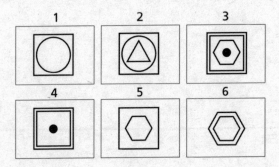

ANSWER:

Puzzle 5.31	Difficulty rating: 2

HEADS OR TAILS?

A box contains two coins. One coin is heads on both sides and the other is heads on one side and tails on the other. One coin is selected from the box at random and the face of one side is observed. If the face is heads what is the percentage chance that the other side is heads?

ANSWER:

Puzzle 5.32	Difficulty rating: 2

MISSING WORD

Complete the comparison:

MONACO is to FRANCE as . . . is to SOUTH AFRICA

A. Eritrea
B. Great Britain
C. Pretoria
D. Lesotho
E. Cape Town

ANSWER:

COMPLETE THE SEQUENCE

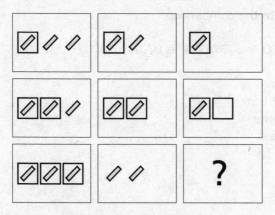

Which one is correct?

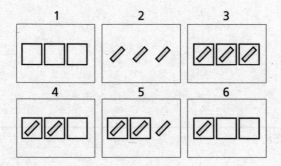

| Puzzle 5.34 | Difficulty rating: 2 |

MISSING WORD

Complete the comparison:

DATUM is to STRATUM as DATA is to . . .

A. Strata
B. Strati
C. Stratums
D. Stratus

ANSWER:

| **Puzzle 5.35** | **Difficulty rating: 1** |

COMPLETE THE SEQUENCE

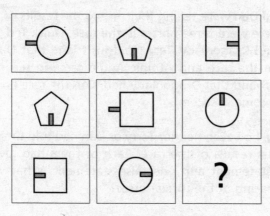

Which one is correct?

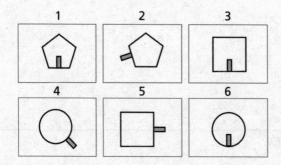

ANSWER:

| Puzzle 5.36 | Difficulty rating: 2 |

HORSE RACE

Terry and Dan were telling their friend the results of a horse race. There were three horses in the race, Quick Ted, Atomic Angie and Dragonlady. Terry told his friend that Quick Ted had won the race and Atomic Angie came in second. Dan told his friend that Dragonlady had won the race and Quick Ted had come in second.

In reality, however, neither Terry or Dan had told their friend the actual results of the race. Each of them had given one correct statement and one false statement. What was the actual placing of the three horses?

ANSWER:

MISSING WORD

Complete the comparison:

GAVRILO PRINCIP is to ARCHDUKE FERDINAND as GUITEAU is to . . .

A. Martin Luther King
B. Charles de Gaulle
C. Marshall Tito
D. Lee Harvey Oswald
E. James Garfield

ANSWER:

Puzzle 5.38	Difficulty rating: 2

CHAPTER 5 ANSWERS

5.1 C. Paper
5.2 Four hours
5.3 Five cars
5.4 2
5.5 B. Scuttle
5.6 99 seconds. Each cut, including the 99th, produces two pieces of wire.
5.7 B. Tine
5.8 3
5.9 1
5.10 B. England
5.11 3
5.12 George slept through half the trip.
5.13 C. Real
5.14 6
5.15 A. Wagon
5.16 4
5.17 Use two vertical cuts to make an X so that you have four pieces, then make a horizontal cut through the cake to make eight pieces.
5.18 B. Obesity
5.19 3
5.20 C. Revolution

5.21 5
5.22 Yes.
       X X O
       X O X
       O X X
5.23 B. League of Nations
5.24 3
5.25 B. Singing
5.26 1
5.27 25 cows would eat all the grass in five days.
5.28 E. Stones
5.29 2
5.30 D. Bullet
5.31 2
5.32 66 per cent
5.33 D. Lesotho
5.34 6
5.35 A. Strata
5.36 2
5.37 Dragonlady won, Atomic Angie came in second and Quick Ted came in third.
5.38 E. James Garfield

6

DIFFICULTY RATING: 76

SPEEDING FINE

Wayne is a delivery man and gets paid $500 for every delivery he makes on time. The only problem is, he has to speed to make the delivery on time. He gets pulled over for speeding 25 per cent of the time, which makes him late for the delivery, which means he doesn't get paid for the delivery, and he has to pay a $200 speeding ticket. How much is Wayne making on average per delivery?

ANSWER:

| Puzzle 6.1 | Difficulty rating: 2 |

MISSING WORD

Complete the comparison:

NORMANDY is to CHAMPAGNE as ONTARIO is to . . .

A. Superior
B. Ardennes
C. Dunkirk
D. Hastings
E. Quebec

ANSWER:

<table>
<tr><td>**Puzzle 6.2**</td><td>**Difficulty rating: 2**</td></tr>
</table>

HOW MANY?

I can buy two Es for one D and one F for one D. I have four Es. How many Fs can I buy?

A. 2
B. 8
C. 16
D. 4

ANSWER:

| Puzzle 6.3 | Difficulty rating: 1 |

BACTERIA

Casey is studying a type of bacteria that multiply every minute. Casey places one bacteria strain in a Petri dish and after one minute the bacteria splits. One minute later the two bacteria split again. One minute after that the four bacteria split and so on. After three hours the dish is half-full. How long will it take to fill the dish completely?

ANSWER:

| Puzzle 6.4 | Difficulty rating: 2 |

COMPLETE THE SEQUENCE

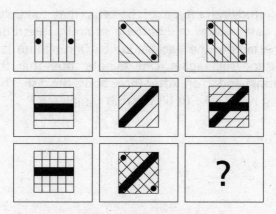

Which one is correct?

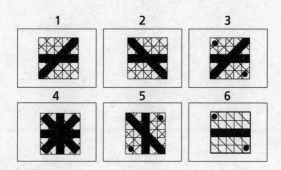

ANSWER:

| Puzzle 6.5 | Difficulty rating: 2 |

210

MISSING WORD

Complete the comparison:

METEOROLOGY is to WEATHER as HOROLOGY is to . . .

A. Horoscopes
B. Food
C. Religion
D. Shape of the skull
E. Time

ANSWER:

Puzzle 6.6	Difficulty rating: 2

COMPLETE THE SEQUENCE

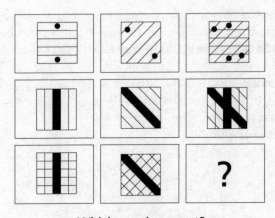

Which one is correct?

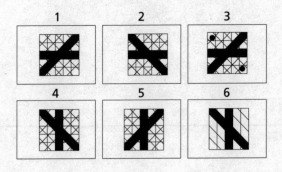

ANSWER:

| Puzzle 6.7 | Difficulty rating: 2 |

JUGGLING

Freckles the clown has just learned how to juggle four balls. How many total throws must he make before the balls are returned to their original positions?

Freckles starts out with two balls in each hand and throws one ball from one hand, then another ball from the second hand, then the remaining ball from the first hand and so on.

ANSWER:

| Puzzle 6.8 | Difficulty rating: 2 |

COMPLETE THE SEQUENCE

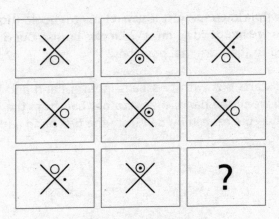

Which one is correct?

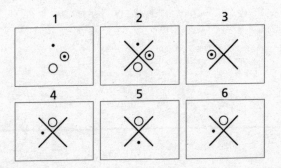

BICYCLES

Two people can make two bicycles in two hours. How many people are needed to make 12 bicycles in six hours?

A. 2
B. 3
C. 4
D. 5
E. 6

ANSWER:

| Puzzle 6.10 | Difficulty rating: 2 |

COMPLETE THE SEQUENCE

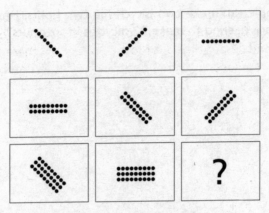

Which one is correct?

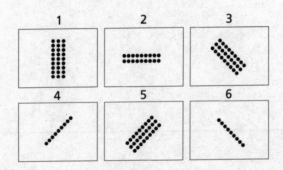

ANSWER:

Puzzle 6.11 | Difficulty rating: 2

HIGH SCHOOL

All of the students at a high school are playing baseball, football or both. 73 per cent of the students are baseball players, and 62 per cent are football players. If there are 200 students, how many of them are playing both baseball and football?

ANSWER:

COMPLETE THE SEQUENCE

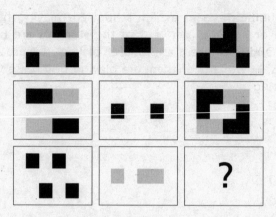

Which one is correct?

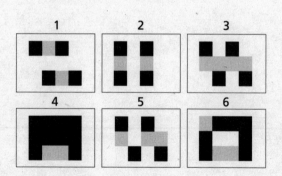

ANSWER:

| Puzzle 6.13 | Difficulty rating: 2 |

MISSING WORD

Complete the comparison:

ICHTHYOPHOBIA is to FISH as SOMNIPHOBIA is to . . .

A. Sleeping
B. Eating
C. Sounds
D. Death
E. Insects

ANSWER:

COMPLETE THE SEQUENCE

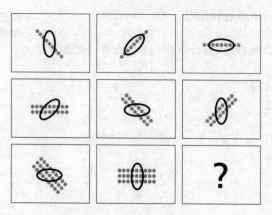

Which one is correct?

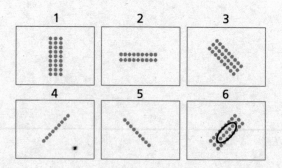

ANSWER:

| Puzzle 6.15 | Difficulty rating: 2 |

SIBLINGS

Each child in the Smith family has at least three brothers and four sisters. What is the smallest number of children the Smith family might have?

ANSWER:

| Puzzle 6.16 | Difficulty rating: 2 |

COMPLETE THE SEQUENCE

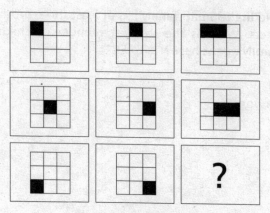

Which one is correct?

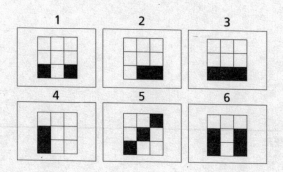

ANSWER:

| Puzzle 6.17 | Difficulty rating: 2 |

MISSING WORD

Complete the comparison:

. . . is to DINNER as NOON is to EVENING

A. Lunch
B. Afternoon
C. Night
D. Snack
E. Food

ANSWER:

| Puzzle 6.18 | Difficulty rating: 2 |

COMPLETE THE SEQUENCE

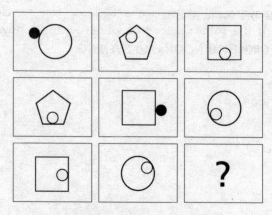

Which one is correct?

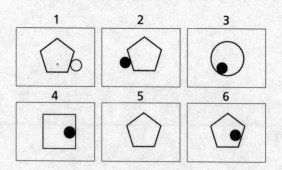

ANSWER:

| Puzzle 6.19 | Difficulty rating: 2 |

WHEELS

At the playground there are a total of ten bicycles and tricycles. If the total number of wheels was 24, how many tricycles were there?

ANSWER:

Puzzle 6.20	Difficulty rating: 2

COMPLETE THE SEQUENCE

Which one is correct?

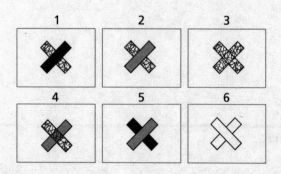

ANSWER:

| Puzzle 6.21 | Difficulty rating: 2 |

MISSING WORD

Complete the comparison:

NORTH STAR is to DOG STAR as POLARIS is to . . .

A. Orion
B. Mercury
C. Ursa
D. Sirius
E. Iridium

ANSWER:

Puzzle 6.22	Difficulty rating: 2

COMPLETE THE SEQUENCE

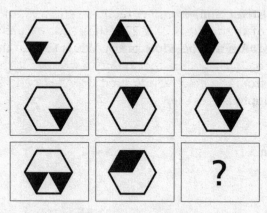

Which one is correct?

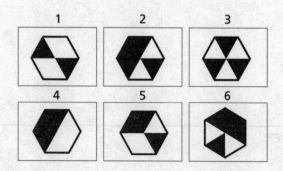

ANSWER:

| Puzzle 6.23 | Difficulty rating: 2 |

TICK TACK

An upholsterer is putting new fabric on the back of a chair. The size of the fabric is 27 x 27 inches and the upholsterer uses tacks all along the edges of the square so that there are 28 tacks on each side of the square. Each tack is the same distance from the neighboring tacks. How many tacks in all does the upholsterer use?

ANSWER:

Puzzle 6.24	Difficulty rating: 2

COMPLETE THE SEQUENCE

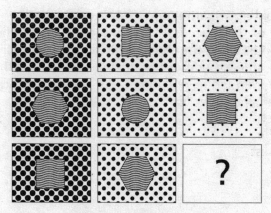

Which one is correct?

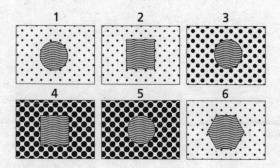

ANSWER:

Puzzle 6.25	Difficulty rating: 2

MISSING WORD

Complete the comparison:

VIENNA is to PRAGUE as WIEN is to . . .

A. Praha
B. Austria
C. Mozart
D. Danube
E. Budapest

ANSWER:

Puzzle 6.26	Difficulty rating: 2

COMPLETE THE SEQUENCE

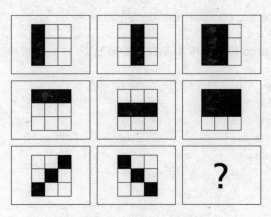

Which one is correct?

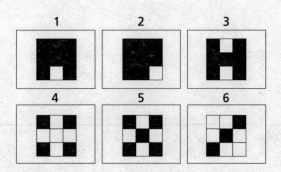

ANSWER:

Puzzle 6.27	Difficulty rating: 2

SCHOOL CHALK

Erin is a teacher at the local elementary school and likes to use chalk. She just bought a pack of 16 sticks. When a stick is three-quarters gone it gets too small for her to use so she stops using it. She found out that when she has enough of these small pieces to make another stick of the same size, she joins them together and adds them back into the box as a new stick. If Erin uses one piece of chalk each day, how many days would her box of 16 last?

ANSWER:

| Puzzle 6.28 | Difficulty rating: 2 |

COMPLETE THE SEQUENCE

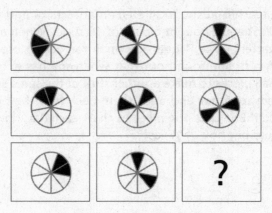

Which one is correct?

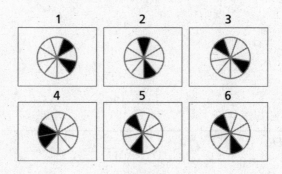

ANSWER:

| Puzzle 6.29 | Difficulty rating: 2 |

MEETING PLACE

To the left are four people located on different squares. They all need to meet up at a specific square. The number underneath each person determines how many horizontal and vertical moves (i.e. straight lines crossing one or more squares) they need to make in order to meet up. Can you find the meeting location?

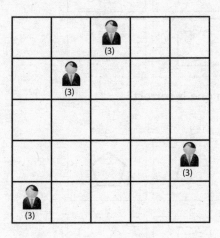

Example:

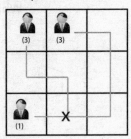

ANSWER:

COMPLETE THE SEQUENCE

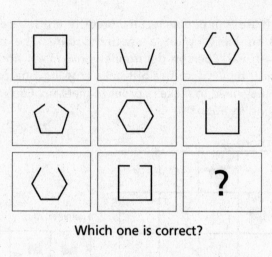

Which one is correct?

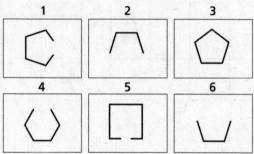

Puzzle 6.31	Difficulty rating: 2

MISSING WORD

Complete the comparison:

CELLO is to VIOLIN as TRUMPET is to . . .

A. Viola
B. Flute
C. Piano
D. Harpsichord

ANSWER:

DIAMOND THEFT

The Cullinan Diamond is the largest diamond in the world. A group of twelve thieves stole it from the Queen of England. During the getaway, however, they dropped the diamond and it broke into seven equal pieces. They took the seven pieces to a jeweler and asked him to divide them evenly, so each of the twelve thieves got an equal amount. How did the jeweler divide the pieces?

ANSWER:

Puzzle 6.33   **Difficulty rating: 2**

COMPLETE THE SEQUENCE

Which one is correct?

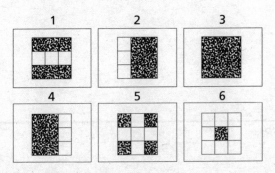

Puzzle 6.34 | **Difficulty rating: 2**

MISSING WORD

Complete the comparison:

PLUMB is to VERTICAL as DIURNAL is to . . .

A. Horizontal
B. Diary
C. Daily
D. Crooked

ANSWER:

| Puzzle 6.35 | Difficulty rating: 2 |

ROPE LADDER

A ship is sitting in port and there is a rope ladder hanging over the side so the people can get on and off the ship. If the tide rises one inch per hour, at the end of five hours how much of the ladder will be remaining above water, assuming that 10 feet were above water when the tide began to rise?

ANSWER:

COMPLETE THE SEQUENCE

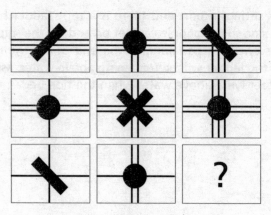

Which one is correct?

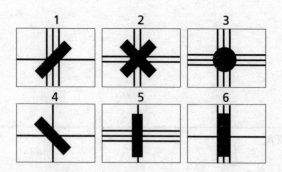

| Puzzle 6.37 | Difficulty rating: 2 |

DESKS AND CHAIRS

Tom sells desks and chairs. The desks cost 25 times as much as the chairs do. Tom sold ten items, and one-fifth of them were desks. If the desks cost $100 for two, how much money did Tom earn?

ANSWER:

CHAPTER 6 ANSWERS

6.1 $325 per delivery
6.2 E. Quebec
6.3 A. 2
6.4 One minute. Remember, they double every minute, so when the dish is half-full, it will only take one more doubling to fill it.
6.5 3
6.6 E. Time
6.7 4
6.8 Eight throws
6.9 6
6.10 C. 4
6.11 5
6.12 35 per cent are playing both for a total of 70 students.
6.13 5
6.14 A. Sleeping
6.15 6
6.16 The smallest number of children the Smith family might have is nine.

6.17 1
6.18 A. Lunch
6.19 2
6.20 Four tricycles in the park.
6.21 1
6.22 D. Sirius
6.23 2
6.24 108 tacks. The four corners of the square have one tack each so each side of the square now requires 26 tacks. The total number of tacks used = 4 + (4 x 26) = 108.
6.25 1
6.26 A. Praha
6.27 5
6.28 21 days. Erin has 16 pieces in the original box. The small pieces make four new pieces and the small pieces of the four new pieces make one more for 21 total.
6.29 6

6.30

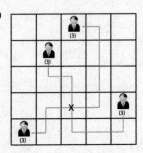

6.31 3

6.32 B. Flute

6.33 He cut four of the pieces into three pieces each and then cut the three remaining pieces into four pieces each, and divided them accordingly.

6.34 5

6.35 C. Daily

6.36 10 feet. The ship will rise with the tide and so will the ladder so it won't affect the amount that is above water.

6.37 1

6.38 $116. Tom sold ten items, and two of them were desks, therefore he sold two desks and eight chairs. Desks cost $50 each, so we know he made $100 from the sale of the desks, and we know he sold eight chairs, which cost 1/25th of the cost of the desk or $2 per chair.

7

DIFFICULTY RATING: 86

DORKS AND ZORGS

If most Gannucks are Dorks and some Gannucks are Xorgs, the statement that some Dorks are Xorgs is:

A. True
B. False
C. Indeterminable from data

ANSWER:

Puzzle 7.1	Difficulty rating: 2

COMPLETE THE SEQUENCE

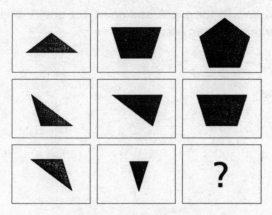

Which one is correct?

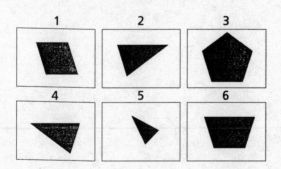

ANSWER:

| Puzzle 7.2 | Difficulty rating: 2 |

249

HOW MANY?

I can buy two Bs for one A and one C for one A. I have four Bs. How many Cs can I buy?

ANSWER:

EMPLOYEES

An office has 27 employees. If there are 7 more women than men in the office, how many employees are women?

ANSWER:

COMPLETE THE SEQUENCE

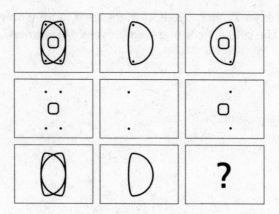

Which one is correct?

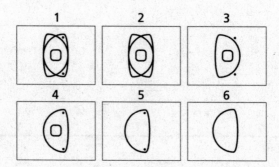

ANSWER:

| Puzzle 7.5 | Difficulty rating: 2 |

SCIENTISTS

All Astronauts are Scientists and some Scientists are Mathematicians. A few Mathematicians are Professors; therefore all Professors are Scientists.

A. True
B. False
C. Indeterminable from data

ANSWER:

| **Puzzle 7.6** | **Difficulty rating: 2** |

MISSING WORD

Complete the comparison:

WEALTHY is to INDIGENT as PARSIMONY is to . . .

A. Frugality
B. Ephemeral
C. Generosity
D. Abstemious

ANSWER:

| Puzzle 7.7 | Difficulty rating: 2 |

WORKFORCE

The local factory's workforce is 20 per cent part-time workers, with the rest of the workers full-time. At the end of the year 30 per cent of the full-time workers received bonuses. If 72 full-time workers received bonuses, how many workers does the factory employ?

ANSWER:

COMPLETE THE SEQUENCE

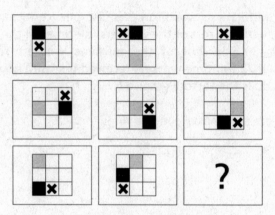

Which one is correct?

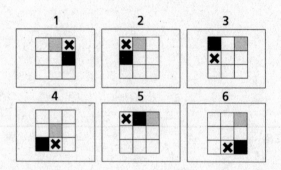

ANSWER:

| Puzzle 7.9 | Difficulty rating: 2 |

ZUGS AND NOGS

Pirs are four times as long as Nogs. Zugs are two times as long as Pirs. That means:

A. Nogs are eight times as long as Zugs
B. Zugs are eight times as long as Nogs
C. Nogs are sixteen times as long as Zugs
D. Zugs are six times as long as Nogs

ANSWER:

MISSING WORD

Complete the comparison:

ACCORD is to BREACH as GAUCHE is to . . .

A. Clandestine
B. Graceful
C. Clumsy
D. Prolix

ANSWER:

FOG HORN

A fog horn sounds regularly five times a minute. A neighboring fog horn blows regularly four times a minute. If they blow simultaneously, after how many seconds will they blow together again?

ANSWER:

COMPLETE THE SEQUENCE

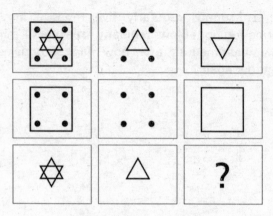

Which one is correct?

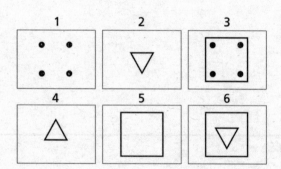

ANSWER:

| Puzzle 7.13 | Difficulty rating: 2 |

CHEESE

Jenny is trying to figure out the weight of a wheel of cheese. She knows that one-fifth of a pound of cheese is perfectly balanced by two-fifths of a wheel of the same cheese. How much does the entire wheel of cheese weigh?

ANSWER:

SETTLE YOUR DEBTS

Alison owes Robert $4, Robert owes Christine $3, and Carol owes Alison $5. If Christine settles all the debts by giving money to both Alison and Robert, how much will she give Alison?

ANSWER:

| **Puzzle 7.15** | **Difficulty rating: 2** |

COMPLETE THE SEQUENCE

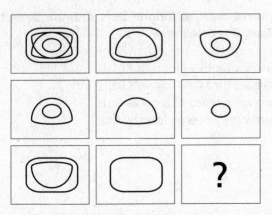

Which one is correct?

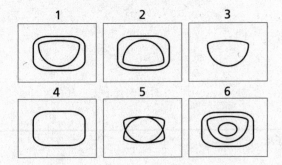

ANSWER:

| Puzzle 7.16 | Difficulty rating: 2 |

CIDS AND BOFS

Rars are three times as long as Bofs. Cids are three times as long as Rars. That means:

A. Cids are six times as long as Bofs
B. Bofs are six times as long as Cids
C. Cids are nine times as long as Bofs
D. Bofs are nine times as long as Cids

ANSWER:

| **Puzzle 7.17** | **Difficulty rating: 2** |

DOG AND CAT

The family dog, Buster, weighs 80 pounds more than Felix, the cat. If their combined weight is 120 pounds, how much does Buster weigh?

ANSWER:

Puzzle 7.18	Difficulty rating: 2

COMPLETE THE SEQUENCE

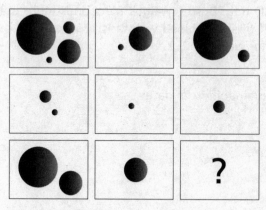

Which one is correct?

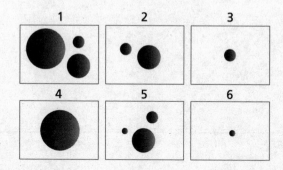

ANSWER:

Puzzle 7.19	Difficulty rating: 2

DORKS AND ZORGS

If all Gannucks are Dorks and some Gannucks are Xorgs, the statement that some Dorks are Xorgs is:

A. True
B. False
C. Indeterminable from data

ANSWER:

| Puzzle 7.20 | Difficulty rating: 2 |

MISSING WORD

Complete the comparison:

LAMP is to LIGHT as SUN is to . . .

A. Dark
B. Night
C. Life
D. Moon
E. Star

ANSWER:

Puzzle 7.21	Difficulty rating: 2

COMPLETE THE SEQUENCE

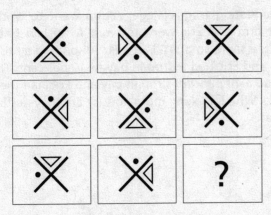

Which one is correct?

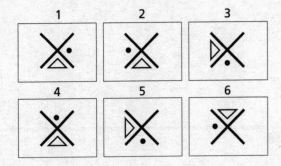

ANSWER:

| Puzzle 7.22 | Difficulty rating: 2 |

WHO EARNS MORE?

After graduating from college, Alison went to work for a financial firm and Eric went to work for a law firm, both earning the same amount. Last year Alison had a raise of 10 per cent and Eric had a drop in pay of 10 per cent. This year Alison had a 10 per cent drop in pay and Eric had the 10 per cent raise. Who is making more now, or are they getting paid the same?

ANSWER:

| Puzzle 7.23 | Difficulty rating: 3 |

COMPLETE THE SEQUENCE

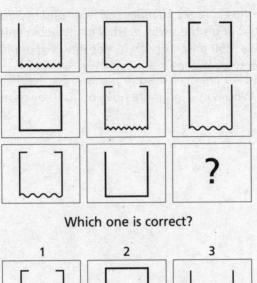

Which one is correct?

1   2   3

4   5   6

ANSWER:

| Puzzle 7.24 | Difficulty rating: 2 |

SUBMARINE

A submarine averages 10 miles per hour under water and 25 miles per hour on the surface. How many hours will it take it to make a 350-mile trip if it goes two-and-a-half times farther on the surface?

ANSWER:

| Puzzle 7.25 | Difficulty rating: 3 |

HOW MANY GAMES?

Patti and Josh decided to play squash against each other, betting ten dollars on each game they played. Patti won three games and Josh won $50. How many games did they play?

ANSWER:

COMPLETE THE SEQUENCE

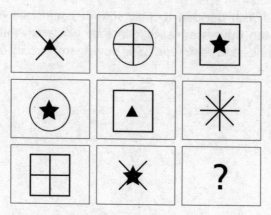

Which one is correct?

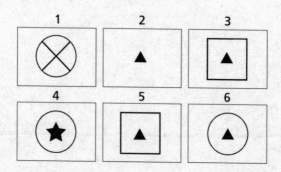

| Puzzle 7.27 | Difficulty rating: 2 |

BASKETBALL

A basketball player shoots 33 per cent from the foul line. How many shots must he take to make 100 baskets?

ANSWER:

| Puzzle 7.28 | Difficulty rating: 3 |

DIGITAL CLOCK

On a digital clock, how many times in a 12-hour period are the numbers displayed in consecutive order (for example, 1:23)?

ANSWER:

| Puzzle 7.29 | Difficulty rating: 3 |

COMPLETE THE SEQUENCE

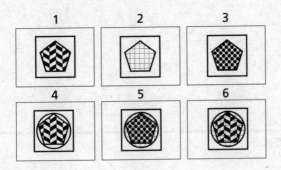

Which one is correct?

ANSWER:

SUSHI

A sushi restaurant buys 20 fish for $10 each. The owner knows that 50 per cent of the fish will go bad before being served. Each fish creates 10 servings. What price must they charge per serving in order to make a 100 per cent profit on their initial investment?

ANSWER:

WORD PUZZLE

Change the first letter of each word to form a new word and place the new letter between the parenthesis to form a new word vertically.

BITE   ( )   PEWS
BEND   ( )   VENT
BUT   ( )   BAT
DOTE   ( )   CASE
BARS   ( )   BASE

ANSWER:

Puzzle 7.32	Difficulty rating: 3

PIE SALE

At the annual baked goods sale Mrs. Ramsey sold 60 pies during the six-day sale. Each day she sold four more pies than she did on the previous day. How many pies were sold on the first day?

ANSWER:

| Puzzle 7.33 | Difficulty rating: 3 |

MISSING WORD

Complete the comparison:

LIMESTONE is to MARBLE as QUARTZ is to . . .

A. Quarry
B. Watch
C. Granite
D. Sedimentary

ANSWER:

Puzzle 7.34	Difficulty rating: 2

BUILD A WALL

If it takes four bricklayers an hour to build a wall, how long will it take five of them to build the same wall?

ANSWER:

MISSING WORD

Complete the comparison:

PART is to WHOLE as UNITED STATES is to . . .

A. North America
B. United Kingdom
C. Okinawa
D. Texas

ANSWER:

DOLPHINS

If it takes five dolphins five minutes to eat five fish, how many minutes would it take four dolphins to eat four fish?

ANSWER:

| Puzzle 7.37 | Difficulty rating: 2 |

CUP OF COFFEE

A bag of coffee beans costs $30 and contains 100 possible servings. However, typical wastage averages 25 per cent. For how much must the proprietor sell a cup of coffee to make 150 per cent profit per bag?

ANSWER:

CHAPTER 7 ANSWERS

7.1 C. Indeterminable from data

7.2 4

7.3 Two Cs

7.4 17. You just need to find two numbers seven apart that add up to 27. With trial and error you should be able to find them soon; 10 and 17; there must be 17 women working at the office.

7.5 6

7.6 C. Indeterminable from data

7.7 C. Generosity

7.8 300. 20 per cent of the workers are part-time, so 80 per cent of the workers are full-time. 30 per cent received bonuses and this amounted to 72 workers. 30 per cent of 80 per cent of total workers (n) equals 72. $3/10 \times 8/10 \times n = 72$, or $24/100 \times n = 72$. Therefore, $n = 72 \times 100/24$, or 300.

7.9 3

7.10 B. Zugs are eight times as long as Nogs.

7.11 B. Graceful

7.12 60. If you convert everything to seconds, the first fog horn blows every 12 seconds and the second fog horn blows every 15 seconds. Then find the lowest common denominator, which is 60, and you arrive at the answer.

7.13 2

7.14 It weighs half a pound. $1/5 \times 5/2 = 5/10$ or $1/2$ pound.

7.15 $1. Christine is owed $3 by Robert, and she owes $5 to Alison. She needs a cash loss of $2 to settle all debts. Alison, on the other hand, is owed $5 by Christine and owes $4 to Robert. She must have a gain of $1. Since Christine settles all debts, this $1 must come from Christine, and this is the answer.

7.16 3

7.17 C. Cids are nine times as long as Bofs.

7.18 Buster weighs 100 pounds and Felix weighs 20 pounds.

7.19 4

7.20 A. True

7.21 C. Life

7.22 1

7.23 They are both making the same

amount. Let's say that in their first year they both earn $10,000. Year two Alison gets a raise to $11,000 and Eric's pay drops to $9,000. Year three Alison's pay drops by 10 per cent and goes to $9,900 while Eric's pay raises 10 per cent and goes from $9,000 to $9,900. They are both now earning $9,900 a year.

7.24   5

7.25   20 hours

7.26   They played 11 games. Josh lost three games; he had to win three additional games to break even; then he had to win five more games to win $50 (3 + 3 + 5 = 11).

7.27   6

7.28   301 shots are required. Due to the 33.333333 phenomenon, he needs to make that 301st shot since you can't throw one-third of a basketball.

7.29   Nine times. 1:23, 2:34, 3:45, 4:56, 9:10, 10:11, 11:12, 12:13, 12:34.

7.30   1

7.31 $4. He spends $200 to buy the 20 fish, but $100 worth goes bad. The remaining $100 worth gives 100 servings and he must charge $4 per serving to reach the 100 per cent profit goal of $400.

7.32   S T O V E
BITE   (S)   PEWS
BEND   (T)   VENT
BUT   (O)   BAT
DOTE   (V)   CASE
BARS   (E)   BASE

7.33   None. 4 + 8 + 12 + 16 + 20 = 60. Because this total is the exact number of pies sold there could not have been any pies sold on the first day.

7.34   C. Granite

7.35   48 minutes. If each bricklayer can put up one brick a minute, then four bricklayers can put up four bricks a minute (240 bricks in an hour's worth of wall building). With five bricklayers they can put up five bricks a minute, and therefore can do the same 240 brick wall in 48 minutes.

7.36   A. North America

7.37   It would still take five minutes for four dolphins to eat four fish.

7.38   60¢. If the bag of coffee costs $30 then the owner needs to make $45 per bag to reach his profit goal. Since he can only get 75 servings from a bag due to wastage he must charge 60¢ a cup.

DIFFICULTY RATING: 111

JELLYBEANS

The local high school was trying to raise money for a class trip by having students pay $1 to guess the number of jellybeans in a jar. Adam guessed 43, Duncan guessed 34, and Carl guessed 41. One person was off by six, another was off by three, and another was off by one. How many jellybeans were in the jar?

ANSWER:

COMPLETE THE SEQUENCE

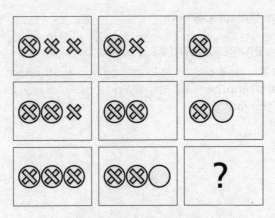

Which one is correct?

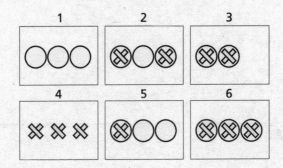

ANSWER:

| Puzzle 8.2 | Difficulty rating: 3 |

MISSING WORD

Complete the comparison:

SILO is to BARREL as WHEAT is to . . .

A. Wine
B. Chaff
C. Staves
D. Casks

ANSWER:

| Puzzle 8.3 | Difficulty rating: 2 |

GOLD BARS

A banker had a scale that was only balanced when there were three gold bars on one side of the scale and one gold bar and a 10 kilogram weight on the other side. Assuming all the gold bars weigh the same amount, how much does one gold bar weigh?

ANSWER:

| Puzzle 8.4 | Difficulty rating: 3 |

COST OF CLOTH

If a pair of pants takes one-and-a-half as much cloth as a shirt, and the total cloth used for the pants and the shirt is $50, how much does the cloth for the pants cost?

ANSWER:

MISSING WORD

Complete the comparison:

HEMMINGWAY is to PLATH as WOOLF is to . . .

A. Thompson
B. Walden
C. Hawthorne
D. Faulkner

ANSWER:

| Puzzle 8.6 | Difficulty rating: 2 |

BUTCHER'S SHOP

Lola's butcher seems to have gone mad. Her ticket says three, but upon closer inspection of the remaining tickets, she can't seem to figure out the numbering. Her butcher assures her there is a logical sequence to the tickets, but he notes that one is out of place – can you find it?

ANSWER:

| Puzzle 8.7 | Difficulty rating: 3 |

CANDIED APPLES

The Moore family had twelve people over for candied apples but they only made seven. How would they divide the seven candied apples among people so that everyone will have exactly equal portions? Each apple cannot be cut into more than four pieces.

ANSWER:

Puzzle 8.8	Difficulty rating: 3

COMPLETE THE SEQUENCE

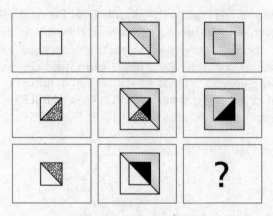

Which one is correct?

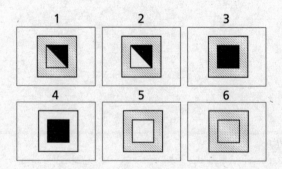

| Puzzle 8.9 | Difficulty rating: 3 |

BOBBLES AND BABBLES

BUBBLES are twice as STRONG as BOBBLES. BABBLES are three times as STRONG as BUBBLES. That means:

A. BOBBLES are six times as STRONG as BABBLES
B. BABBLES are eight times as STRONG as BOBBLES
C. BOBBLES are eight times as STRONG as BABBLES
D. BABBLES are six times as STRONG as BOBBLES

ANSWER:

| Puzzle 8.10 | Difficulty rating: 3 |

MINING FOR GOLD

There is a golden block hidden in the grid. Use the numbered blocks to locate the hidden block. Blocks with numbers in them indicate how many blocks away from the hidden square they are. You cannot move diagonally, and each block you pass through counts as one. You are permitted to travel through numbered squares, but the hidden block cannot occupy a numbered square.

In the example the block with the number three in it passes through three empty squares before reaching the golden square.

Example

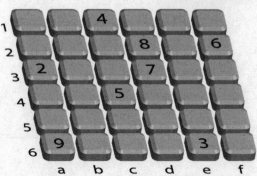

ANSWER:

Puzzle 8.11	Difficulty rating: 3

WEEDS

Mary Ellen and Barbara both have equal sized gardens in their front yard. Barbara decides to plant a single weed in Mary Ellen's garden so it won't look as nice. The weed doubles every day and within 30 days Mary Ellen's garden is completely covered in weeds. If we assume the weed doubles in number every day, how many days will it take Barbara's garden to be completely covered in weeds when Mary Ellen plants two weeds in her garden?

ANSWER:

| Puzzle 8.12 | Difficulty rating: 3 |

CLOCK PUZZLE

If the minute hand has just passed the hour hand how long will it take until the next time this happens?

ANSWER:

COMPLETE THE SEQUENCE

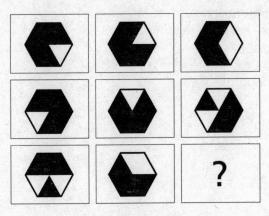

Which one is correct?

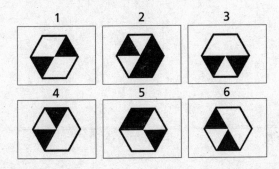

ANSWER:

| Puzzle 8.14 | Difficulty rating: 3 |

NUMBER SEQUENCE

What comes next?

1, 6, 14, 30, 62 . . .

A. 130
B. 126
C. 200
D. 900

ANSWER:

<table>
<tr><td>**Puzzle 8.15**</td><td>**Difficulty rating: 3**</td></tr>
</table>

SQUARE PUZZLE

How many squares are there in the following image?

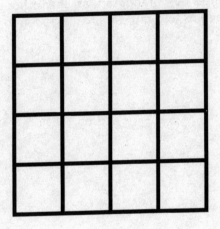

ANSWER:

| Puzzle 8.16 | Difficulty rating: 3 |

ORANGUTAN

A weightless and perfectly flexible rope is hung over a weightless, frictionless pulley attached to the roof of a building. At one end is a weight which exactly counterbalances an orangutan at the other end. If the orangutan begins to climb, what will happen to the weight?

ANSWER:

COMPLETE THE SEQUENCE

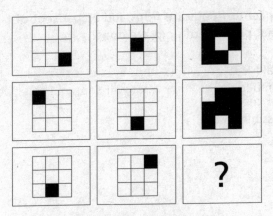

Which one is correct?

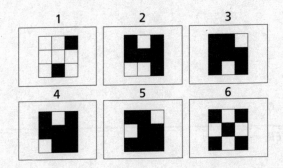

POGS AND NOGS

If 50 per cent of pogs are frogs and 25 per cent of frogs are Nogs, what per cent of pogs are nogs?

A. 12.5 per cent
B. 25 per cent
C. 50 per cent
D. Impossible to tell

ANSWER:

| Puzzle 8.19 | Difficulty rating: 3 |

HOW OLD?

Fred and Duncan were at a party and people were trying to guess how old they were. Instead of telling them how old each was, Duncan said, "Our ages add up to 55, and Fred's age is my age in reverse." How old are Fred and Duncan?

ANSWER:

Puzzle 8.20	Difficulty rating: 3

COMPLETE THE SEQUENCE

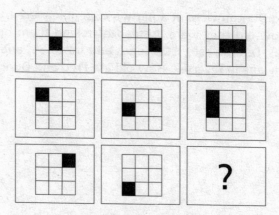

Which one is correct?

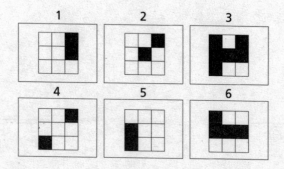

ANSWER:

| Puzzle 8.21 | Difficulty rating: 3 |

HOW OLD?

Joe is one and one-third older than Marty, or half as old as Hector. Hector is 16. How old is Marty?

A. 6
B. 2
C. 3
D. 7

ANSWER:

| Puzzle 8.22 | Difficulty rating: 3 |

STAMPS

Using a strip of four stamps, how many ways can you fold the stamps into a flat pile, without tearing the perforations? Hint: With a strip of three stamps, there are six unique ways to fold the strip.

ANSWER:

| Puzzle 8.23 | Difficulty rating: 3 |

HANDBAGS

Trish was looking in her closet, trying to figure out how many handbags she owned. All her bags are gold except two. All her bags are brown except two. All her bags are white except two. How many handbags does Trish have?

ANSWER:

COMPLETE THE SEQUENCE

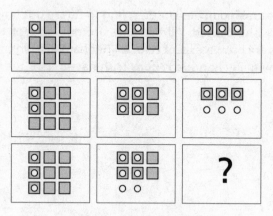

Which one is correct?

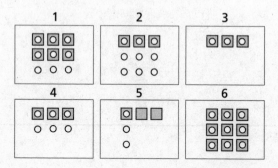

ANSWER:

Puzzle 8.25	Difficulty rating: 3

314

MISSING WORD

Complete the comparison:

JAI ALAI is to . . . as BICYCLE is to VELODROME

A. Aztec
B. Court
C. Mexico
D. Track
E. Fronton

ANSWER:

Puzzle 8.26	Difficulty rating: 3

HORSE RACE

COMP   ENCE

Toby was an eccentric man who decided to give his fortune away to the winner of a horse race. In the rules, the winner was the one who came in last, but Toby didn't want the race to last forever so he came up with an answer. What was it?

ANSWER:

| Puzzle 8.27 | Difficulty rating: 3 |

COMPLETE THE SEQUENCE

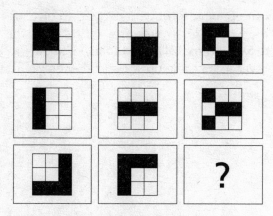

Which one is correct?

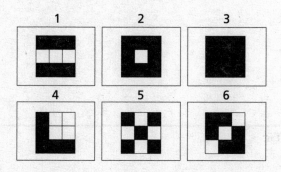

ANSWER:

| Puzzle 8.28 | Difficulty rating: 3 |

MISSING WORD

Complete the comparison:

MARS is to SATURN as POLARIS is to . . .

A. Sirius
B. North Star
C. Rings
D. Jupiter
E. Galileo

ANSWER:

EXPRESS TRAIN

Every hour on the hour a train leaves Boston for New York and a train leaves New York for Boston.

The trains all travel at the same speed and the trip from Boston to New York takes five hours. How many trains pass by each other on one trip?

ANSWER:

Puzzle 8.30	Difficulty rating: 3

COMPLETE THE SEQUENCE

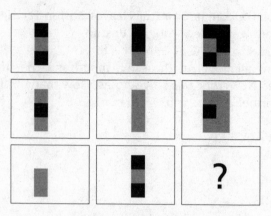

Which one is correct?

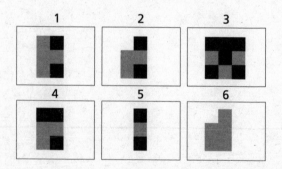

ANSWER:

Puzzle 8.31	Difficulty rating: 3

MISSING WORD

Complete the comparison:

UNICORN is to DODO as GRIFFIN is to . . .

A. Horse
B. Dragon
C. Pegasus
D. Great Auk
E. Icarus

ANSWER:

Puzzle 8.32	Difficulty rating: 3

CONFERENCE

For an international summit 15 representatives from the United States, France, Britain and Germany met in Switzerland. Each country sent a different number of representatives and each country is represented by at least one person. Britain and France sent a total of six representatives. France and Germany sent a total of seven representatives. Which country sent four representatives?

ANSWER:

Puzzle 8.33	Difficulty rating: 3

COMPLETE THE SEQUENCE

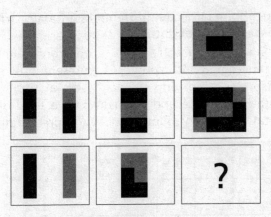

Which one is correct?

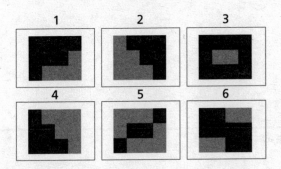

ANSWER:

| Puzzle 8.34 | Difficulty rating: 3 |

DOTTY

Can you fill in the question-marked boxes with the appropriate number of dots?

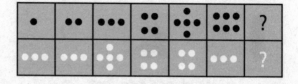

ANSWER:

| Puzzle 8.35 | Difficulty rating: 3 |

JOURNEY

Duncan and Lorraine are preparing to take a 4,000-mile trip in their car. The car has four tires and each tire only lasts 1,500 miles. How many tires will Duncan and Lorraine go through if we assume the tires on the car are brand new?

ANSWER:

| Puzzle 8.36 | Difficulty rating: 3 |

COMPLETE THE SEQUENCE

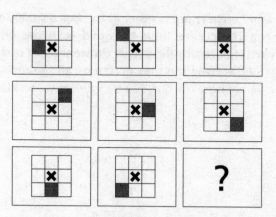

Which one is correct?

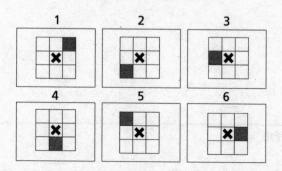

Puzzle 8.37	Difficulty rating: 3

DINNER PARTY

Three people are having a dinner party. Blake shows up with five dishes and his friend Brian brings three dishes. Jodi stops by with no dishes but decides to sit down and eat with them. Jodi pays $20 as her share. If we assume all the dishes have the same value, how can the $20 be split between Blake and Brian?

ANSWER:

| Puzzle 8.38 | Difficulty rating: 3 |

CHAPTER 8 ANSWERS

8.1   40 jellybeans in the jar

8.2   5

8.3   A. Wine

8.4   By removing one gold bar from each side of the scale, two gold bars weigh 10 kilograms total. Therefore one gold bar weighs 5 kilograms.

8.5 $30. It takes 1.5 square feet for the pants, and 1 for the shirt, for 2.5 sq ft of cloth for both, making the cost per sq ft at $20. $20 x 1.5 = $30 for the pants and $20 for shirt.

8.6   A. Thompson

8.7   Ten. The numbers are in alphabetical order.

8.8   Cut four of the apples into three pieces each and then cut the three remaining apples into four pieces each.

8.9   1

8.10   D. BABBLES are six times as STRONG as BOBBLES.

8.11   b5

8.12   29 days. The doubling still occurs each day, we can just rule out the first day since it was doubled initially.

8.13   1 hour and 5 minutes

8.14   6

8.15   B. 126 (2 + 1 x 2 = 6, 6 + 1 x 2 = 14...)

8.16   30. There are 16 one-by-one squares, 9 two-by-two squares (watch out, they overlap!), 4 three-by-three squares and 1 large four-by-four square, giving a total of 30 squares in all.

8.17   The weight will rise with the orangutan.

8.18 3

8.19 A. 12.5 per cent

8.20 Fred is 41 and Duncan is 14.

8.21 4

8.22 A. 6

8.23 There are 16 unique folds for a strip of 4 stamps.

8.24 Trish has three handbags, one gold, one brown, and one white.

8.25 2

8.26 E. Fronton

8.27 Toby made each person ride another person's horse, which would ensure that everyone would want to come in first so they wouldn't lose.

8.28 6

8.29 A. Sirius

8.30 11 trains. Trains pass by every half hour (nine trains total), plus two pulling into the cities.

8.31 2

8.32 D. Great Auk

8.33 France

8.34 4

8.35 The top row should have seven dots and the bottom row should have five. The bottom row of dots represents the number of letters used to spell the number of dots in the top row.

8.36 12 tires. After 1,500 miles all four tires need changing; after 3,000 miles it's eight tires used; up to 4,000 miles it's a third set of four (part used); 3 x 4 = 12.

8.37 3

8.38 Total cost of meal is: 3 people x $20 = $60. Eight dishes have been eaten, therefore each dish costs $7.50. Blake brought 5 dishes x $7.50 = $37.50 minus his $20 share or $17.50. Brian brought 3 dishes x $7.50 minus his share = $2.50.

9

DIFFICULTY RATING: 115

CHICKENS AND GOATS

In the barnyard there are goats and chickens. In all, there are 22 heads and 72 feet. How many chickens and goats are there in the barnyard?

ANSWER:

| Puzzle 9.1 | Difficulty rating: 3 |

COMPLETE THE SEQUENCE

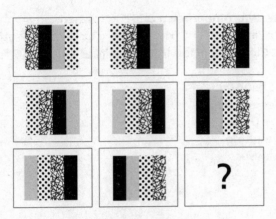

Which one is correct?

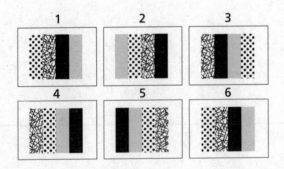

| Puzzle 9.2 | Difficulty rating: 3 |

MISSING WORD

Complete the comparison:

SAMUEL CLEMENS is to MARK TWAIN as ERIC BLAIR is to . . .

A. John Steinbeck
B. Huckleberry Finn
C. George Orwell
D. Stephen King
E. Tom Sawyer

ANSWER:

Puzzle 9.3	Difficulty rating: 3

CEGS AND KAMS

Some Fors are Kams and all Fors are Zops. Most Zops are Cegs, therefore a few Cegs are Kams.

A. True
B. False
C. Indeterminable from data

ANSWER:

| Puzzle 9.4 | Difficulty rating: 3 |

COMPLETE THE SEQUENCE

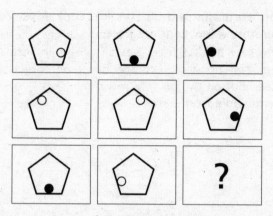

Which one is correct?

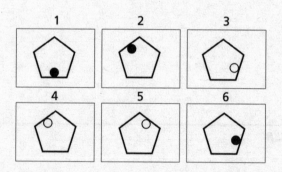

| Puzzle 9.5 | Difficulty rating: 3 |

BUILDING BLOCKS

Little Tricia is playing with blocks in her room. She decides to stack up all the blocks so that each row has one less block than the row below. Tricia has 55 blocks in total and she wants to end up with just one block on top. How many should she put on the bottom row?

ANSWER:

| Puzzle 9.6 | Difficulty rating: 3 |

DON'T BE SQUARE

Below there is a large square made up of four shapes, and a separate square (shown as letter E) to the side. Using all five of the shapes (A through E) only once, form a second perfect square.

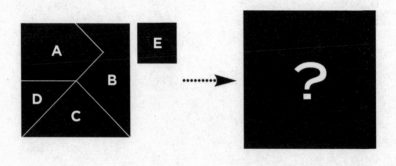

ANSWER:

| Puzzle 9.7 | Difficulty rating: 3 |

MISSING WORD

Complete the comparison:

BIBLIOPHILE is to BOOKS as OENOPHILE is to . . .

A. Wine
B. Foreigners
C. Perfume
D. Smell
E. Masks

ANSWER:

Puzzle 9.8	Difficulty rating: 3

COMPLETE THE SEQUENCE

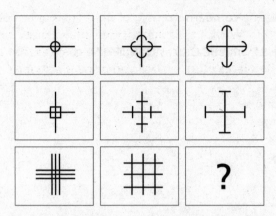

Which one is correct?

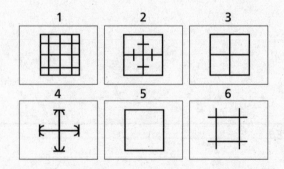

SPOONS AND FORKS

Sharon has two boxes, each box holding four spoons and four forks. Without looking, you draw one piece of silverware from each box. What are the chances that at least one of the pieces of silverware you draw is a spoon?

ANSWER:

MEETING PLACE

To the left are three people located on different squares. They all need to meet up at a specific square. The number underneath each person determines how many horizontal and vertical moves (i.e. straight lines crossing one or more squares) they need to make in order to meet up. Can you find the meeting location?

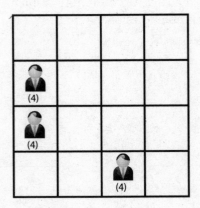

Example:

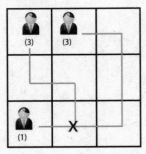

ANSWER:

| Puzzle 9.11 | Difficulty rating: 3 |

ASSASSINATION

Josh is in charge of protecting two diplomats during a summit, one from France and one from Britain. Josh has a 25 per cent chance of thwarting an assassination attempt against the French diplomat and a 50 per cent chance of thwarting an assassination attempt against the British diplomat. If there are 6 people at the summit who are going to attempt to assassinate the French diplomat and 10 people attempting to assassinate the British diplomat, which diplomat is in greater danger of being assassinated?

ANSWER:

| Puzzle 9.12 | Difficulty rating: 3 |

COMPLETE THE SEQUENCE

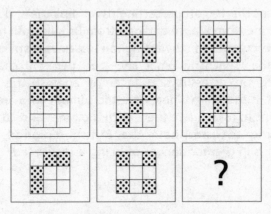

Which one is correct?

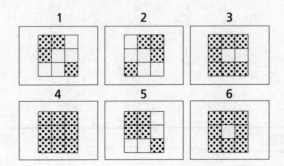

ANSWER:

| Puzzle 9.13 | Difficulty rating: 3 |

344

LOST PROPERTY

In a group of 100 students, 70 lost a notebook, 75 lost a pencil, 85 lost a calculator, and 80 lost a ruler. What is the minimum number of students who must have lost all four?

ANSWER:

ORANGES

Michael had a job at the produce stand stacking the oranges. His boss told him to stack 35 oranges so that each row of oranges would have one more than the row above it. How many rows of oranges did Michael have when he was finished?

ANSWER:

| Puzzle 9.15 | Difficulty rating: 3 |

MISSING WORD

Complete the comparison:

HAMLET is to MACBETH as MERCHANT OF VENICE is to . . .

A. Othello
B. Romeo and Juliet
C. Taming of the Shrew
D. Julius Caesar
E. King Lear

ANSWER:

| Puzzle 9.16 | Difficulty rating: 3 |

COMPLETE THE SEQUENCE

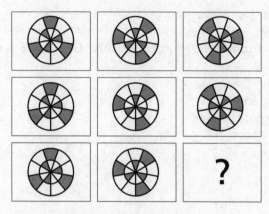

Which one is correct?

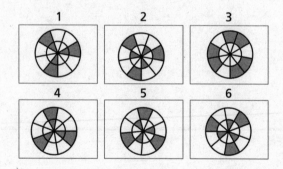

Puzzle 9.17	Difficulty rating: 3

HOW OLD?

Lauren is twice as old as her brother and half as old as her father. In 22 years, her brother will be half as old as his father. How old is Lauren now?

ANSWER:

MISSING NUMBER

What number should replace the question mark?

15	2	11	8
5	1	4	?
3	12	6	7
7	9	21	2

ANSWER:

Puzzle 9.19	Difficulty rating: 3

BRICK WALL

Dominic and his brother can build a wall five bricks long and five bricks high in one minute. How long will it take them to build a wall ten bricks long and ten bricks high?

ANSWER:

COMPLETE THE SEQUENCE

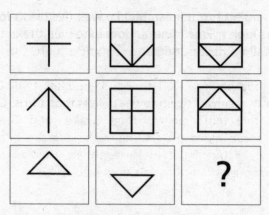

?

Which one is correct?

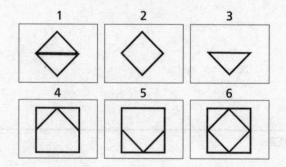

| Puzzle 9.21 | Difficulty rating: 3 |

MOUSE MAZE

Andy, Duncan, Chris, Drake, and Eric are mice learning to go through a maze. Each time a mouse reaches the end of the maze, it gets a pellet of food.

So far, Andy has received four more pellets than Duncan. Duncan has received seven fewer pellets than Chris. Chris has received five more pellets than Drake, and Drake has received three more pellets than Eric. Duncan and Drake have received ten pellets between them. How many times has each mouse gone through the maze so far?

ANSWER:

MISSING WORD

Complete the comparison:

SEATO is to MANILA as LEAGUE OF NATIONS is to . . .

A. New York
B. Precursor
C. Treaty
D. Versailles
E. NATO

ANSWER:

| Puzzle 9.23 | Difficulty rating: 3 |

SHOE SALE

Tommy and Ralph both own clothing stores selling the same items. Tommy sells the same pair of shoes as Ralph, and they both sell for $100. Tommy decides to lower the price by 25 per cent and Ralph counters by lowering the price 30 per cent. When Tommy finds out Ralph lowered the price on his shoes, Tommy lowered the price of his by another 15 per cent. Ralph in turn lowered the price of his by 10 per cent. Who is selling the shoes for the cheapest?

ANSWER:

| **Puzzle 9.24** | **Difficulty rating: 3** |

HATS

Two people can make two hats in two hours. How many people are needed to make 12 hats in six hours?

ANSWER:

COMPLETE THE SEQUENCE

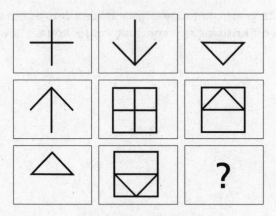

Which one is correct?

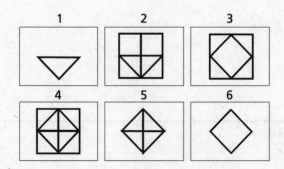

ANSWER:

HOW OLD?

Chris is 33 years old today. This is three times as old as Paul was when Chris was the age that Paul is today. How old is Paul?

ANSWER:

MISSING WORD

Complete the comparison:

PAINTER is to CANVAS as LAPIDARY is to . . .

A. Gems
B. Acrylic
C. Gallery
D. Appraisal
E. Pencil

ANSWER:

Puzzle 9.28	Difficulty rating: 3

SINGING LESSONS

Anthony, Duncan, Carl, and Dave all decided to start taking singing lessons. Carl took twice as many lessons as Duncan. Anthony took four lessons more than Dave but three fewer than Carl. Dave took 15 lessons altogether. How many singing lessons did Duncan take?

ANSWER:

Puzzle 9.29	Difficulty rating: 3

COMPLETE THE SEQUENCE

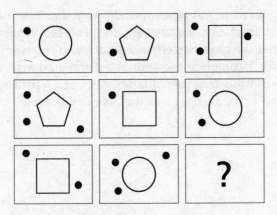

Which one is correct?

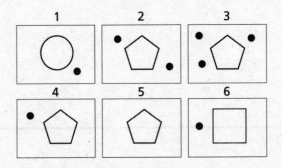

ANSWER:

Puzzle 9.30	Difficulty rating: 3

JIGSAW PUZZLE

Candace loved to put jigsaw puzzles together. She managed to try at least one puzzle per day. For every puzzle she completed she gave herself two points, and for every puzzle she couldn't complete she subtracted three points. After 30 days of putting together puzzles, Candace had a score of zero. How many puzzles was she able to complete?

ANSWER:

| **Puzzle 9.31** | **Difficulty rating: 3** |

COMPLETE THE SEQUENCE

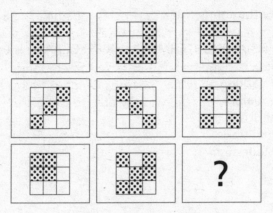

Which one is correct?

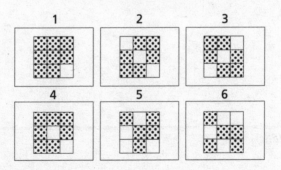

| Puzzle 9.32 | Difficulty rating: 3 |

MISSING WORD

Complete the comparison:

HOBBES is to ENLIGHTENMENT as KIERKEGAARD is to . . .

A. Reformation
B. Existentialism
C. Romanticism
D. Creationism
E. Post Modernism

ANSWER:

CAR SALE

A car dealership reduced the price of one of its models by 25 per cent for it's Year End Sale. By what percentage of the sales price must it be increased to put the car back to its original price?

ANSWER:

COMPLETE THE SEQUENCE

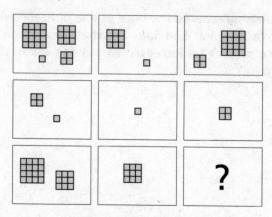

Which one is correct?

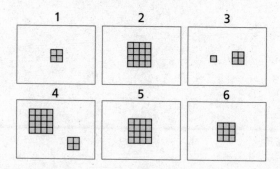

ANSWER:

Puzzle 9.35	Difficulty rating: 3

MISSING WORD

Complete the comparison:

SILICON is to ARSENIC as IODINE is to . . .

A. Chlorine
B. Radon
C. Germanium
D. Bismuth
E. Poison

ANSWER:

Puzzle 9.36	Difficulty rating: 3

BROTHERS

Jack has six brothers. Each brother is four years older than his next younger brother. The oldest brother is three times as old as his youngest brother. How old are each of the brothers?

ANSWER:

TRIANGLE PUZZLE

Using only three cuts, dissect the triangle and form the square.

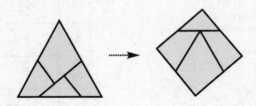

ANSWER:

| **Puzzle 9.38** | **Difficulty rating: 3** |

CHAPTER 9 ANSWERS

9.1 Eight chickens and 14 goats.

9.2 3

9.3 C. George Orwell

9.4 C. Indeterminable from data

9.5 4

9.6 Ten blocks

9.7

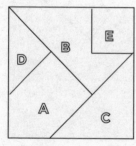

9.8 A. Wine

9.9 3

9.10 There are four possibilities: 1 spoon and 1 fork / 2 spoons / 1 fork and 1 spoon / 2 forks. In three of the four possibilities, you'll wind up with at least one spoon. So the chances of picking at least one spoon are 3 in 4 or, in another phrasing, 3 to 1.

9.11

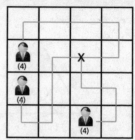

9.12 The British diplomat is in greater danger than the French diplomat (50 per cent x 10 = five assassination attempts on the British diplomat are likely to succeed compared to 25 per cent x 6 = one and a half assassination attempts on the French diplomat are likely to succeed).

9.13 1

9.14 If you add up all the losses you find that 100 students lost a total of 310 items. That total means that, at a minimum, 100 students lost three items, and 10 (the remainder when dividing 310 by 100) must have lost all four items.

9.15 Seven rows. Eight oranges in the bottom row, two in the top.

9.16 C. Taming of the Shrew

9.17 2

9.18 Lauren is 22 years old.

9.19 17. In each vertical column the three smaller numbers equal the larger number.

9.20 Four minutes. The first wall has 25 bricks. The second wall has four times as many, so it will take four times as long, or four minutes.

9.21 2

9.22 Andy has gone through eight times, Duncan four times, Chris eleven times, Drake six times, Eric three times.

9.23 D. Versailles

9.24 Ralph. Tommy is selling the shoes for $63.75 and Ralph is selling them for $63.

9.25 Four people can make 12 hats in six hours.

9.26 3

9.27 22 years old

9.28 A. Gems

9.29 Duncan took 11 lessons.

9.30 4

9.31 Candace solved 18 puzzles correctly, earning 36 points. She failed to solve 12 correctly, losing 36 points.

9.32 2

9.33 B. Existentialism

9.34 If the car originally cost $30,000, with the 25 per cent deduction, it would cost $22,500. To bring the price back to the original $30,000, you'd have to add $7,500, which is one-third of $22,500, or 33.3 per cent.

9.35 2

9.36 A. Chlorine

9.37 From youngest to oldest, the six brothers are 10, 14, 18, 22, 26 and 30.

9.38

371

10

DIFFICULTY RATING: 124

FACTORY WORK

Trent, Mary and Shawn all work in a factory. Trent earns half of what Mary makes. Shawn earns three times what Trent makes. If the three of them together earn $144 a day, how much are each of them making in a day?

ANSWER:

COMPLETE THE SEQUENCE

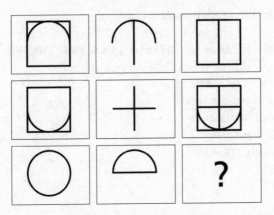

Which one is correct?

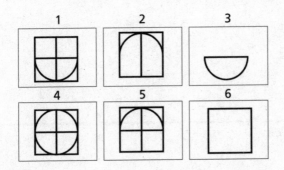

MISSING WORD

Complete the comparison:

GALVANOMETER is to CURRENT as KATHAROMETER is to . . .

A. Atmosphere pressure
B. Thermal conductivity
C. Electrical resistance
D. Blood pressure
E. Radiation pressure

ANSWER:

Puzzle 10.3	Difficulty rating: 3

If ten hens can produce 15 eggs in a week, how many eggs can 15 hens produce in two weeks?

ANSWER:

Puzzle 10.4	Difficulty rating: 3

COMPLETE THE SEQUENCE

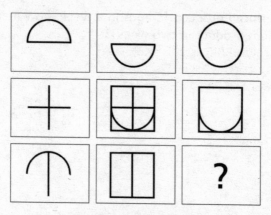

Which one is correct?

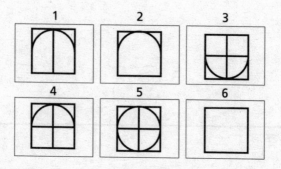

ANSWER:

MISSING WORD

Complete the comparison:

103 is to LOCKERBIE as 007 is to . . .

A. James Bond
B. MI5
C. England
D. Sea of Japan
E. Korean

ANSWER:

MEETING PLACE

To the left are three people located on different squares. They all need to meet up at a specific square. The number underneath each person determines how many horizontal and vertical moves (i.e. straight lines crossing one or more squares) they need to make in order to meet up. Can you find the meeting location?

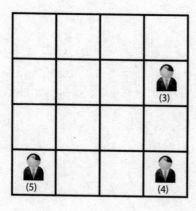

Example:

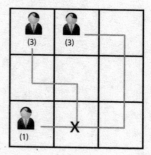

ANSWER:

Puzzle 10.7	Difficulty rating: 3

WATER JUGS

Using a garden hose, how can you measure out one liter of water, if all you have available is a 3-liter and a 5-liter jug?

ANSWER:

| Puzzle 10.8 | Difficulty rating: 3 |

COMPLETE THE SEQUENCE

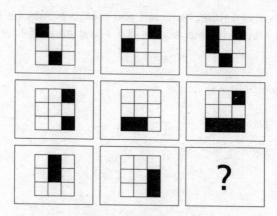

Which one is correct?

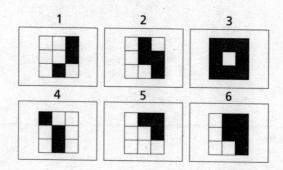

ANSWER:

| Puzzle 10.9 | Difficulty rating: 4 |

MISSING WORD

Complete the comparison:

RGB is to CMYK as DIGITAL is to . . .

A. Analog
B. Print
C. Color spectrum
D. ROYGBIV
E. Electronic

ANSWER:

Puzzle 10.10	Difficulty rating: 3

RIVER CROSSING

A man goes to an auction and buys a wolf, a goat and a bag of grain. When he leaves the auction he starts walking home. To get home, he must cross a river, but he's only allowed to take one item across the bridge with him at a time. If he leaves the wolf with the goat, the wolf will eat the goat. If the goat is left alone with the grain, the goat will eat the grain. How can the man cross the river without any of his possessions being eaten?

ANSWER:

Puzzle 10.11	Difficulty rating: 3

SUMMER HOME

The Merriweathers, the Milkens, the Weills, and Ivan are buying a summer home in the Hamptons. They all decide to divide the purchase price according to who earns the most money. The house costs $66,000. The Milkens earn the most and will pay one third of the cost. The Merriweathers will pay three times what Ivan will pay and twice the amount that the Weills will pay. How much will everyone have to pay?

ANSWER:

COMPLETE THE SEQUENCE

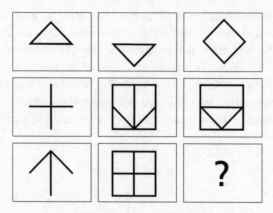

Which one is correct?

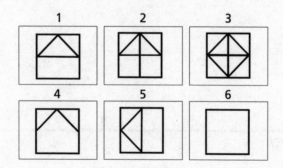

ANSWER:

| Puzzle 10.13 | Difficulty rating: 4 |

MISSING WORD

Complete the comparison:

CREPUSCULAR is to DIM as QUIDNUNC is to . . .

A. Testator
B. Theorist
C. Quisling
D. Busybody

ANSWER:

| Puzzle 10.14 | Difficulty rating: 3 |

HAPPY HOUR

It's time for one of Lola's famous martini parties, but she only has two tables in her apartment. One table seats eight, the other six. Lola invites all 13 of her friends, and they never decline. If all 14 girls want to sit with everyone, how many parties do the girls have to attend?

ANSWER:

| Puzzle 10.15 | Difficulty rating: 3 |

ROOFERS

Tim and Greg are roofers. Tim makes $100 a day and Greg makes $75 a day. If they just finished a roofing job in which they charged the customer $1,000 for labor, how many days did they work on the roof?

ANSWER:

COMPLETE THE SEQUENCE

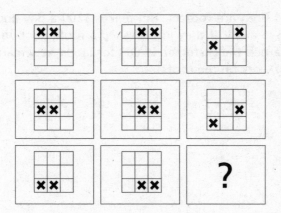

Which one is correct?

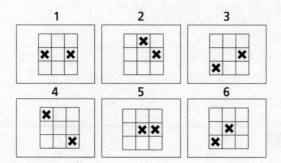

ANSWER:

Puzzle 10.17 | **Difficulty rating: 4**

MISSING WORD

Complete the comparison:

SOUND is to TASTE as HEAR is to . . .

A. Color
B. Smell
C. Food
D. Ear

ANSWER:

| Puzzle 10.18 | Difficulty rating: 3 |

RACE RESULTS

Pete showed up at the local race track just after the first race ended. He asked his buddy Brad what the results of race were, and Brad said:

Silver Wagon finished before Master David and after Say it Fast. Say it Fast tied with Silver Wagon if and only if Sir Oscar did not tie with Lion Heart. Silver Wagon finished as many places after Lion Heart as Lion Heart finished after Say it Fast if and only if Say it Fast finished before Master David. How did the five horses finish the race?

ANSWER:

| Puzzle 10.19 | Difficulty rating: 3 |

OFFICE STAPLES

Jim needs to buy 100 staplers for his company with a budget of $100. He has to buy exactly 100 staplers and he must use the entire $100. If the jumbo staplers cost $6, the regular staplers cost $3, and the tiny staplers cost 10¢, how many of each does Jim have to buy?

ANSWER:

Puzzle 10.20	Difficulty rating: 3

COMPLETE THE SEQUENCE

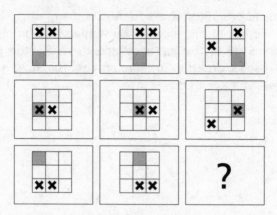

Which one is correct?

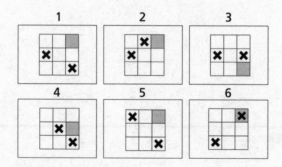

ANSWER:

Puzzle 10.21 | **Difficulty rating: 4**

MISSING WORD

Complete the comparison:

CADUCEUS is to SCALES as DOCTOR is to . . .

A. Justice
B. Medicine
C. Sophocles
D. Lawyer

ANSWER:

| Puzzle 10.22 | Difficulty rating: 3 |

CLOTHES SWAP

Daren, Tom, Rob and Matt went to a black-tie benefit. When they arrived, they checked their coats, hats, gloves and canes at the door (each of the gentlemen had one of each). When they checked out, there was a mix up, and each of the men ended up with exactly one article of clothing belonging to each one of the four. Daren and Tom ended up with their own coats, Rob ended up with his own hat, and Matt ended up with his own gloves. Daren did not end up with Rob's cane. Whose coat, hat, gloves, and cane did each of the gentlemen end up with?

ANSWER:

STAR GAZING

The six-pointed star below has six lines and 12 vertices. Can you arrange the numbers 1 through 12, so that each line adds up to 26?

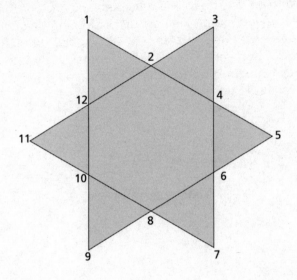

ANSWER:

Puzzle 10.24 | **Difficulty rating: 3**

BACK TO SCHOOL

Laura went back-to-school shopping and spent half her money on a new jacket. She then spent half of that amount on a pair of sneakers. If she was left with $25, how much did she spend?

ANSWER:

COMPLETE THE SEQUENCE

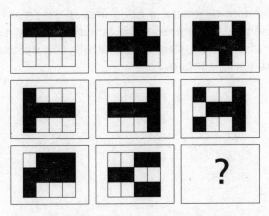

Which one is correct?

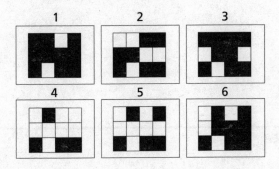

ANSWER:

Puzzle 10.26	Difficulty rating: 4

HOW MUCH?

Nico purchased a camera, a ruler, and an ice cream bar for $53.00. He paid $52 more for the camera than the ice cream bar, and the ruler cost twice as much as the ice cream bar. What did he pay for each?

ANSWER:

MISSING WORD

Complete the comparison:

GHENT is to P'ANMUNJOM as SHIMONOSEKI is to . . .

A. Maastricht
B. Hubertusburg
C. Nanking
D. Okinawa
E. Manila

ANSWER:

Puzzle 10.28	Difficulty rating: 4

HOURGLASS

Using just a four-minute hourglass and a seven-minute hourglass, how can you figure out how to measure out exactly nine minutes?

ANSWER:

| Puzzle 10.29 | Difficulty rating: 3 |

COMPLETE THE SEQUENCE

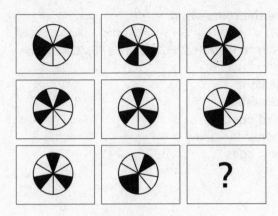

Which one is correct?

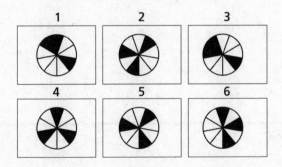

ANSWER:

| Puzzle 10.30 | Difficulty rating: 4 |

MISSING WORD

Complete the comparison:

ROYGBIV is to COLOR SPECTRUM as PEMDAS is to . . .

A. Visible light
B. Periodic table
C. Order of operations
D. Taxonomic hierarchy
E. Geologic ages

ANSWER:

Puzzle 10.31	Difficulty rating: 4

RECTANGLES

What number should replace the question mark?

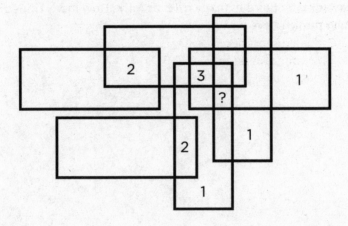

ANSWER:

RIFLES

Duncan and Mick are both collectors of Bedouin rifles. If Duncan were to sell Mick seven rifles, then Duncan would have exactly as many rifles as Mick. On the other hand, if Mick were to sell Duncan seven rifles, then Duncan would have exactly twice as many rifles as Mick. How many rifles did each person have?

ANSWER:

| Puzzle 10.33 | Difficulty rating: 3 |

COMPLETE THE SEQUENCE

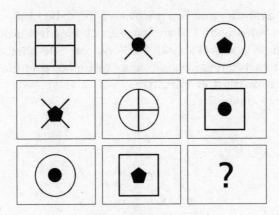

Which one is correct?

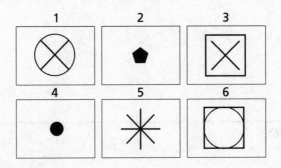

| Puzzle 10.34 | Difficulty rating: 4 |

RANCHER

You are a rancher and you are given $100 to buy 100 animals. You must spend all $100 and have no change left over. Cows cost $10, Pigs cost $5, and Chickens cost 50¢ apiece. How many of each animal do you have to buy to spend all $100 and have exactly 100 animals?

ANSWER:

MATCHBOX CARS

Gary and Jim each have a collection of matchbox cars. Gary said that if Jim would give him nine cars they would have an equal number; but, if Gary would give Jim nine of his cars, Jim would have four times as many cars as Gary. How many matchbox cars does Jim have?

ANSWER:

PEANUTS

Robert can eat 100 peanuts in half a minute, and Matthew can eat half as many in twice the length of time. How many peanuts can Robert and Matthew eat in 15 seconds?

ANSWER:

COMPLETE THE SEQUENCE

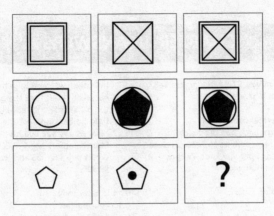

Which one is correct?

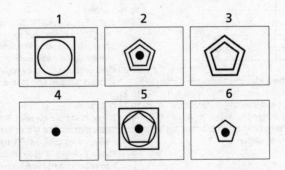

ANSWER:

| Puzzle 10.38 | Difficulty rating: 4 |

CHAPTER 10 ANSWERS

10.1 Trent makes $24, Mary makes $48, Shawn makes $72.

10.2 3

10.3 B. Thermal conductivity

10.4 45 eggs. Each hen produces 1.5 eggs per week, so 15 hens produce 22.5 eggs per week, or 45 eggs in a two week stretch.

10.5 2

10.6 D. Sea of Japan

10.7

10.8 Fill the 3-liter jug and pour it into the 5-liter jug. Fill the 3-liter jug again and add the water to the same 5-liter jug, filling it to the top. What's left in the 3-liter jug is 1 liter of water.

10.9 2

10.10 B. Print

10.11 Take the goat across and leave it on the other side. Then go back and get the wolf and bring it to the other side and take the goat back with you. Take the grain to the other side and leave it there, then go back and get the goat.

10.12 Milkens pay $22,000, the Merriweathers pay $24,000, the Weills pay $12,000 and Ivan pays $8,000.

10.13 1

10.14 D. Busybody

10.15 Four parties

10.16 1,000 divided by $175 is 5.7, so they worked on the roof for 6 days.

10.17 4

10.18 C. Food

10.19 Say it Fast came in first. Lion Heart and Sir Oscar tied for second place. Silver Wagon came in fourth. Master David came in fifth.

10.20 One jumbo stapler, 29 regular staplers, and 70 tiny staplers.

10.21 5

10.22 D. Lawyer

10.23 Daren had his own coat, Tom's hat, Rob's gloves, and Matt's cane. Tom had his own coat, Matt's hat, Daren's gloves, and Rob's cane. Rob had Matt's coat, his own hat, Tom's gloves, and Daren's cane. Matt had Rob's coat, Daren's hat, his own gloves and Tom's cane.

10.24 There are 160 correct solutions. Here's one of them. How many can you find?

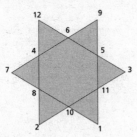

10.25 $75
10.26 4
10.27 Answer: Camera: $52.25
Ruler: $0.50
Ice cream bar: $0.25
10.28 B. Hubertusburg
10.29 Flip both hourglasses over. When the four-minute hourglass runs out, flip it back over immediately. When the seven-minute hourglass runs out, flip that back over immediately too. One minute later, the four-minute hourglass will run out again. At this point, flip the seven-minute hourglass back over. The seven-minute hourglass will have only been running for a minute, so when it is flipped over again it will only run for a minute more before running out. When it does, exactly nine minutes will have passed.
10.30 6
10.31 C. Order of operations
10.32 Three. The numbers represent the numbers of rectangles they are inside.
10.33 Duncan had 49 rifles and Mick had 35. We know from part one of the puzzle that Duncan had seven more rifles than Mick, and we know from part two that if Mick sold seven to Duncan, his collection would be double. Therefore, we need to find the lowest common denominator of seven to make the puzzle work, which is 49 and 35.
10.34 5
10.35 You buy one cow, nine pigs, and 90 chickens.
10.36 Jim has 39 cars and Gary has 21 cars.
10.37 62.5 peanuts
10.38 6

11

DIFFICULTY RATING: 128

SCOTCH BARRELS

Mr McFadden is the recently deceased former owner of a distillery. In his will, he left 21 barrels of scotch (seven of which are filled, seven of which are half full, and seven of which are empty) to his three sons. However, the scotch and barrels must be split so that each son has the same number of full barrels, the same number of half-full barrels, and the same number of empty barrels. If there are no measuring devices handy, how can the barrels and scotch be evenly divided?

ANSWER:

| Puzzle 11.1 | Difficulty rating: 3 |

MEETING PLACE

To the left are three people located on different squares. They all need to meet up at a specific square. The number underneath each person determines how many horizontal and vertical moves (i.e. straight lines crossing one or more squares) they need to make in order to meet up. Can you find the meeting location?

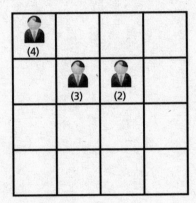

Example:

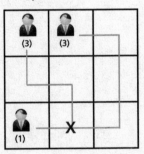

ANSWER:

BUFFET

Albert, Bob, and Carl are eating at an all-you-can-eat buffet. Albert made 2.4 times as many trips to the buffet as Bob, and Bob made six fewer trips than Carl. What is the smallest possible total number of trips the three made to the buffet, assuming that each person made at least one trip?

ANSWER:

CASINO

A casino uses only $5 and $8 chips on its standard roulette wheel. What is the largest wager that cannot be placed?

ANSWER:

SNAIL PACE

A snail is at the bottom of a ten-foot well. He climbs three feet a day, but during the night, while resting, he slips back two feet. At this rate, how many days will it take the snail to climb out of the well?

ANSWER:

FLAGPOLE

There is a flagpole in the middle of Lake Winnipesauke. Half of the flagpole is in the ground, another one-third of it is covered by water, and 10 feet of the flagpole is sticking out of the water. What is the total length of the flagpole?

ANSWER:

| Puzzle 11.6 | Difficulty rating: 3 |

POOL GAME

During his five turns with the cue, a pool player sank 100 balls. During each turn he sank six more balls than he did during his previous turn. Can you figure out how many balls he sank during each of his five turns?

ANSWER:

| Puzzle 11.7 | Difficulty rating: 3 |

MISSING WORD

Complete the comparison:

NIKKEI is to JAPAN as HANG SENG is to . . .

A. London
B. South Korea
C. Yuan
D. Hong Kong
E. Taiwan

ANSWER:

| Puzzle 11.8 | Difficulty rating: 4 |

MEETING POINT

Rochester and Syracuse are 88 miles apart. If Eric leaves Rochester on a bicycle traveling ten miles per hour and Alison leaves Syracuse on foot, traveling one mile per hour, how many miles will Eric have to travel before meeting Alison on the way?

ANSWER:

Puzzle 11.9	Difficulty rating: 3

BASEBALL

In a regular nine-inning baseball game, what is the minimum number of pitched balls that a pitcher, who works the whole game, can throw? Which team is the pitcher on, the home team or the visiting team? The visitors bat first. The answer is neither 27 or 24.

ANSWER:

| Puzzle 11.10 | Difficulty rating: 3 |

HOW OLD?

Joan spent one-quarter of her life as a girl, one-eighth as a youth, and one-half as an adult. If Joan spent ten years as an old woman, how old is she?

ANSWER:

| **Puzzle 11.11** | **Difficulty rating: 3** |

EXAMS

Stephen just finished all four final exams for the semester. He found out that his average score was 81. He also found out that his average in Physics and Math was 78. What was his average score for English and History?

ANSWER:

ARCHERY

Josh and Brian were both champion archers. They decided to put a target 100 yards away and see who could hit the center first. They decided to alternate shots until someone hit the bull's-eye. It was so far away, though, that they only hit the target half the time. If Josh shoots first, what are the odds of him winning the contest?

ANSWER:

| Puzzle 11.13 | Difficulty rating: 3 |

PLASMA TV

A store raised the price of their plasma TVs by 25 per cent for the holidays. After the shopping season was over they lowered the price by 25 per cent. Is the price of the TV lower than before, the same, or more expensive?

ANSWER:

| **Puzzle 11.14** | **Difficulty rating: 3** |

MEETING PLACE

To the left are four people located on different squares. They all need to meet up at a specific square. The number underneath each person determines how many horizontal and vertical moves (i.e. straight lines crossing one or more squares) they need to make in order to meet up. Can you find the meeting location?

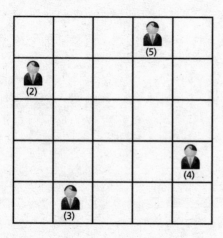

Example:

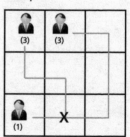

ANSWER:

| Puzzle 11.15 | Difficulty rating: 3 |

BASEBALL LEAGUE

During the Little League baseball season every team plays every other team in the league ten times. If there are ten teams in the league, how many games are played in the league in one season?

ANSWER:

Puzzle 11.16 | **Difficulty rating: 3**

WELL DRESSED

Jonathan finds that by wearing different combinations of the jackets, shirts and pairs of pants that he owns, he can make up 90 different outfits. If he owns five jackets and three pairs of pants, how many shirts does he own?

ANSWER:

| Puzzle 11.17 | Difficulty rating: 3 |

POOL TABLES

Jason starts his own online business selling pool tables and he wants to hire the Federal Express to ship the pool tables. FedEx has two trucks that can handle a pool table, one large and one small. Their large truck is twice as high, twice as wide, and twice as long as their small one. FedEx has decided to charge $500 per shipment for each delivery they make with a fully loaded small truck.

Assuming that charges are based on each truck's volume, what should FedEx charge for each delivery they make with a fully loaded large truck?

ANSWER:

SUBWAY WHEELS

The New York City subway system buys wheels for the subway cars for $200 per wheel. The wheels last for ten years and then they have a scrap value of $25 apiece. If rust-proofing treatment costing $50 a wheel is applied, each wheel will last fifteen years but will have no scrap value. In the long run, would it be more cost effective to rust-proof the wheels or not?

ANSWER:

BOOK CLUB

Tricia, Kelly, Sasha and Meredith start a book club that meets once a month. Each month, one person hosts the party and another person brings the snacks. The host gets to pick the book and one of the other three have to bring the snacks. The responsibility of the hosts and the provider of snacks changes every month. How many months will it take until there has been every possible combination of host and snack provider?

ANSWER:

| Puzzle 11.20 | Difficulty rating: 4 |

WEIGHING SCALES

One shoe weighs eight ounces. If one umbrella is equal to one book plus one shoe, and five books are equal to one umbrella plus one shoe, and one hat is equal to one umbrella plus one book, then how much do the umbrella, book, and hat each weigh?

ANSWER:

ODD WORD OUT

If A = 1, B = 2, and so on.
Which word doesn't belong?

A CAT FINGER BRAT

A. A
B. CAT
C. FINGER
D. BRAT

ANSWER:

COMPLETE THE SEQUENCE

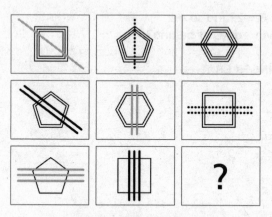

Which one is correct?

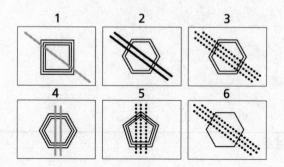

ANSWER:

Puzzle 11.23	Difficulty rating: 3

438

SHOOTING ODDS

Both Aaron and Alexander are average marksmen and only hit their target 50 per cent of the time. They decide to fight a duel in which they exchange alternate shots until one is hit. What are the odds of the man who shoots first?

ANSWER:

| **Puzzle 11.24** | **Difficulty rating: 4** |

A rowboat is floating in a swimming pool. What will raise the level of the water in the pool higher, dropping a marble in the pool or in the rowboat?

ANSWER:

| **Puzzle 11.25** | **Difficulty rating: 4** |

NEWSPAPERS

At a local town hall meeting there was a poll to see what newspapers the citizens were reading. 64 per cent were reading the Sun-Times, 22 per cent were reading the Post and 7 per cent were reading both. What percentage of the citizens polled were reading no newspaper?

ANSWER:

Puzzle 11.26	**Difficulty rating: 3**

SONS AND DAUGHTERS

If each of Peter's sons has twice as many sisters as brothers and each of his daughters has just as many sisters as brothers, how many sons and daughters does Peter have?

ANSWER:

SHOPAHOLIC

Trish decided to go on a shopping spree. At the shoe store she spent half of what she had plus $6 for a pair of boots. At the clothing store she spent half of what was left plus $4 for a scarf. At the candy store she spent half of what remained plus $2 for an ice cream cone. She had $7 left over. How much did she have originally?

ANSWER:

COMPLETE THE SEQUENCE

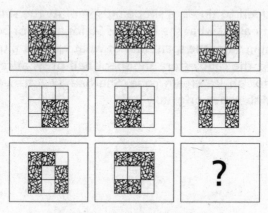

Which one is correct?

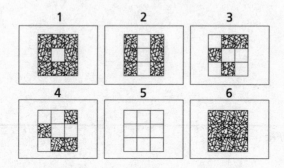

ANSWER:

| Puzzle 11.29 | Difficulty rating: 4 |

444

CHRISTMAS PARTY

At the company's Christmas party, one-third of the employees left early. Later on in the evening, two-fifths of the remaining employees left the party, and a few hours later two-thirds of the remaining employees went home. If there are six employees still at the party, how many attended?

ANSWER:

| Puzzle 11.30 | Difficulty rating: 3 |

CAR PARK

On a busy night the valet parked 320 cars. Twenty per cent of the customers tipped him $1, half of the remaining 80 per cent tipped him $2, and the rest did not tip at all. How much money did the valet make?

ANSWER:

MISSING WORD

Complete the comparison:

GINI COEFFICIENT is to INCOME INEQUALITY as HERFINDAHL INDEX is to ...

A. Opportunity cost
B. Industry concentration
C. Economy of scale
D. Supply and demand curve
E. General equilibrium

ANSWER:

| Puzzle 11.32 | Difficulty rating: 4 |

MOVIES

Four friends decide to go out to the movies. When they arrive there are four empty seats in the theater. How many different combinations are there for the number of ways the four friends could sit in these seats?

ANSWER:

| Puzzle 11.33 | Difficulty rating: 3 |

While running a 3,000-meter race on an indoor track, Joseph notices that one-fifth of the runners in front of him plus five-sixths of the runners behind him add up to the total number of runners. How many people are running in the race?

ANSWER:

Puzzle 11.34	**Difficulty rating: 4**

CIGARETTE BUTT

With the price of cigarettes skyrocketing, Danny figured out that if he collected cigarette butts, he could make a cigarette from every five butts found. He found 25 butts, so how many cigarettes could he smoke?

ANSWER:

COMPLETE THE SEQUENCE

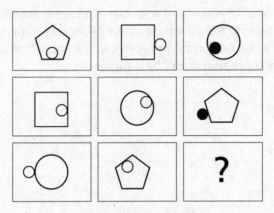

Which one is correct?

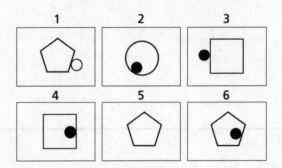

ANSWER:

| Puzzle 11.36 | Difficulty rating: 4 |

451

HARVARD

At Harvard University there are 4,215 freshmen, 3,401 sophomores, 1,903 juniors and 1,757 seniors. One student will randomly be chosen to receive an award. What per cent chance is there that it will be a junior?

ANSWER:

| Puzzle 11.37 | Difficulty rating: 3 |

MOUNT EVEREST

Eric decides to climb Mount Everest with the help of sherpas. It will take him six days to reach the summit, but he can only carry four days' worth of food in his pack. If the sherpas can also only carry four days' worth of food, how many sherpas will Eric need to reach the summit?

ANSWER:

CHAPTER 11 ANSWERS

11.1 Two half-full barrels are dumped into one of the empty barrels. Two more half-full barrels are dumped into another one of the empty barrels. This results in nine full barrels, three half-full barrels, and nine empty barrels. Each son gets three full barrels, one half-full barrel and three empty barrels.

11.2
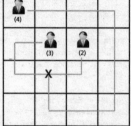

11.3 There were 28 total trips made, with Albert making 12 of them, Bob making 5, and Carl making 11.

11.4 $27 dollars. $28 dollars and above can be made with the combination of $5 and $8 chips.

11.5 Eight days. The snail makes one foot of progress every 24 hours. So after seven days, he will have climbed seven feet. Then on day eight, he will climb the three feet he manages per day and gets out of the well.

11.6 60 feet

11.7 During his five turns at the table he sank 8, 14, 20, 26, and 32 balls.

11.8 D. Hong Kong

11.9 Together they cover the distance at 11 miles per hour so they will cover the distance of 88 miles in eight hours. In eight hours they will meet and Eric will have traveled 80 miles.

11.10 25 pitches. 24 pitches that result in outs and one for a home run to end the game. The pitcher would be on the visiting team.

11.11 Joan is 80 years old. Joan spends 20 years as a girl, 10 years as a youth, and 40 years as an adult and 10 years as an old woman. 20 + 10 + 40 + 10 = 80 years old.

11.12 84 was the average. Total marks in four exams = 4 x 81 = 324. Total marks for Physics and Math = 2 x 78 = 156. Total marks in English and History = 324 - 156 = 168. Average marks in English and History = 168 ÷ 2 = 84 .

11.13 Josh has a two-thirds chance of hitting the bull's-eye before Brian does. The first archer's inital shot hits half the time. If he misses, and the next guy also misses, the first shooter goes again, so for the first three shots the first shooter makes two of them, or two-thirds of the total. Even if they keep missing, the two-thirds statistic remains in effect.

11.14 The price of the TV is less than it was before the 25 per cent increase and the 25 per cent decrease. If the TV cost $1,000 you know that 25 per cent of 1,000 is 250. So, after the 25 per cent increase, the cost was $1,250. Now find 25 per cent of $1,250. Subtract this amount ($312.50) from $1,250 to find the reduced price. It's $937.50 — that's $62.50 less than the original price of $1,000.

11.15

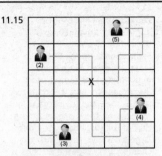

11.16 450. In the ten team league, each team plays the other nine teams ten times each. 9 x 10 = 90 games per team per season. With ten different teams, we arrive at 900 total games played. Then we divide this by two since there are two teams playing in each game. 900 ÷ 2 = 450.

11.17 Six shirts. For every pair of pants, he can wear 5 different jackets, giving 5 different combinations for each pair of pants, or 3 x 5 = 15 different combinations of pants and jackets. With each of these combinations he can wear any of his different shirts. The different combinations of shirts, jackets and pants is (number of shirts) ÷ 15. We are told this equals 90, so 90 divided by 15 equals 6.

11.18 FedEx should charge $4,000 for a large truckload. Since each dimension of the large truck (height, width, and length) is twice that of the small truck, the volume of the large truck is eight times that of the small truck. So, for a large truckload, FedEx should charge eight times the price of a small truckload. That's 8 x $500, or $4,000.

11.19 It would be more cost effective to get the rust-proofing done. Without the rust-proofing the cost is $17.50 per wheel per year and with the rust-proofing the cost is $16.66 per wheel per year.

11.20 12 months. When one person is host, three other people could be the snack provider. Each person gets a chance to be host for three months, each month with a different snack provider. In total there are 12 different host/snack combinations.

11.21 The umbrella weighs 12 ounces, the book 4 ounces, and the hat 16 ounces.

11.22 D. BRAT. If a = 1, b = 2 and so on, "brat" is the only word that has too many letters for it's starting letter placement. A word starting with "b", using this system, should only have two letters.

11.23 6

11.24 The first shooter has a two-thirds chance of hitting his opponent first. The first shooter's first shot hits half the time, so if he misses, and the next guy also misses, the first shooter goes again, so for the first three shots the first shooter makes two of them, or two-thirds of the total. Even if they keep missing, the two-thirds statistic remains in effect.

11.25 Dropping it in the rowboat. Since the marble is denser than water, dropping it into the rowboat will raise the water level higher. Try substituting a marble for a fully-inflated balloon. If you managed to push the balloon underwater it would raise the water level considerably higher than if you dropped the balloon into the rowboat.

11.26 21 per cent. 64 + 22 − 7 = 79. 100 − 79 is 21.

11.27 Three sons and four daughters.

11.28 She started with $100. In the first store she spent $56 and had $44 left. In the second store she spent $26 and had $18 left. At the third store she spent $11 and had $7 left.

11.29 4

11.30 45. There are 45 people, so with 15 leaving early (one-third) this leaves 30 at the party. Then 12 leave (two-fifths), so there are 18 remaining, then two-thirds of these leave (12), giving you the remaining 6 at the party.

11.31 $320. 20 per cent tipped him $64 and half the remaining 80 per cent that tipped $2 gave him $256, for a total of $320.

11.32 B. Industry concentration

11.33 24.

11.34 31 runners in total. Since the track is a closed circuit we simply add $1/5$ + $5/6$ = $31/30$. 30 runners plus Joseph.

11.35 Six cigarettes. Danny made five cigarettes from the 25 butts, smoked them, and then made an additional cigarette from the five butts that were left from the five that he made.

11.36 3

11.37 17 per cent. Divide the number of juniors (1,903) by the total number of students (11,276).

11.38 Eric can reach the summit using only two sherpas. The three of them leave base camp, each with four days' worth of food. At the end of the first day, they all have three days' worth of food left. The first sherpa leaves two days of food with Eric and the other sherpa and heads back to base camp with one day worth of food in his pack. The second day the last sherpa heads back to base camp after leaving one days' worth of food with Eric. Eric now has four days of food and only four days left to get to the summit. He will die of starvation on the way down though.

12

DIFFICULTY RATING: 156

CASH

Tommy goes to the bank to cash his $1,500 paycheck but the bank is missing certain bills. The teller cashes Tommy's check using a certain number of $1 bills, ten times as many $5 bills, and a certain number of $10 bills and twice as many $50 bills. How many bills of each kind does the teller pay out?

ANSWER:

Puzzle 12.1	Difficulty rating: 4

DIM SUM

A bowl of dim sum contains 40 noodles and is split between two people. Each person can take between one and six noodles per bite. If the first person to take a bite wants to guarantee he eats the last bite as well, how many noodles would he eat on his first bite?

ANSWER:

| Puzzle 12.2 | Difficulty rating: 4 |

GOLD COINS

You are given five identical sacks containing ten gold coins in each sack. All the gold coins weigh one pound each except for the coins in the fifth sack. In the fifth sack all the gold coins weigh nine-tenths of a pound.

How can you figure out which sack has the lighter coins in it using a single-tray scale and you are only allowed to use the scale once?

ANSWER:

| Puzzle 12.3 | Difficulty rating: 4 |

COOKING CLASS

Jean-Pierre opened his first French cooking class, and he has fewer than 500 students. One-third of the students is a whole number. So are one-quarter, one-fifth, and one-seventh of the students. How many students are enrolled in Jean-Pierre's cooking class?

ANSWER:

| Puzzle 12.4 | Difficulty rating: 4 |

HOW FAR?

Peter had to drive from New York to Philadelphia but he wasn't in much of a hurry. On the first day he drove one-quarter of the distance, on the second day he drove one-half of the remaining distance, and on the third day he drove three-quarters of the remaining distance. The next day he drove one-third of the remaining distance. He still has 21 miles left to travel. How far is it from New York to Philadelphia?

ANSWER:

| **Puzzle 12.5** | **Difficulty rating: 4** |

PROPOSAL

Brian decided to propose to Andrea. At the first jewelry store he found a one-carat ring for $3,000. At the second jewelry store he found the same one-carat ring for $3,500. The first jewelry store had a 20 per cent fee for any rings that were returned and the second jewelry store had no fees for returns. If there is a 50 per cent chance that Andrea will say no, which jewelry store should Brian buy the ring at to maximize his risk/reward?

ANSWER:

| Puzzle 12.6 | Difficulty rating: 4 |

TUG-OF-WAR

The local high school has an annual tug-of-war game between the sports players. With three football players on one side and two baseball players on the other side, the game ended in a tie. Similarly, with three soccer players on one side and four baseball players on the other side, the game ended in a tie. Which side, if either, will win if one side has five football players and the other side has two soccer players?

ANSWER:

NEW YORK

Vince drove from Atlantic City to New York at the rate of 20 miles an hour. When he got to New York he realized he had forgot his wallet and rushed home at 40 miles an hour. The whole trip took him six hours. How many miles is it from Atlantic City to New York?

ANSWER:

Puzzle 12.8	Difficulty rating: 4

ROULETTE

Carlos is playing roulette in Las Vegas. If there are 36 numbers on the wheel, work out on which two-digit number Carlos has picked, given the following facts: The number is divisible by 3. The sum of the digits in this number lies between 4 and 8. It is an odd number. When the digits in this number are multiplied together, the total lies between 4 and 8.

ANSWER:

| Puzzle 12.9 | Difficulty rating: 4 |

MEGA SHOP

At the MegaloMart wholesale shopping market they sell large containers of orange juice and apple juice. On the shelves there are six containers, each holding the following amounts:

Container A: 30 quarts
Container B: 32 quarts
Container C: 36 quarts
Container D: 38 quarts
Container E: 40 quarts
Container F: 62 quarts

Five of the containers hold orange juice, and one container holds apple juice.

Two customers come into the market and the first customer buys two containers of orange juice. The second customer buys twice as much orange juice as the first customer. Which container is holding the apple juice?

ANSWER:

HOW TALL?

Duncan, Tricia and Lauren are siblings, but they differ greatly in their heights. Tricia is 14 inches taller than Lauren. The difference between Tricia and Duncan is two inches less than between Duncan and Lauren. At 6 foot 6 inches Tricia is the tallest. How tall are Duncan and Lauren?

ANSWER:

Puzzle 12.11	Difficulty rating: 4

FOOTBALL DESIGN

The new FIFA World Cup 2048 football design has been unveiled, unfolded and labeled.

When refolded which letter would be opposite the letter B, and which number would be opposite the number 16?

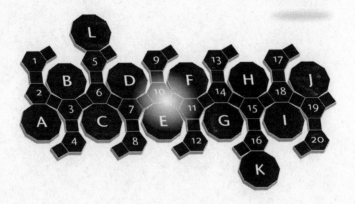

ANSWER:

LONG DRIVE

Justine is planning to drive across the country. She is going to drive a few miles on the first day and add 20 more miles, on each subsequent day, to the number of miles she had traveled the day before. The total trip is going to take her 1,080 miles. How many miles did she drive on the last day?

ANSWER:

| Puzzle 12.13 | Difficulty rating: 4 |

BRIDGE PLAYERS

Five retirees met every week for a game of bridge. They used a table with six chairs. If they had chosen a different seating arrangement each week and had exhausted every possibility, how long had the retirees played bridge together?

ANSWER:

FISH MARKET

At the Fulton Street Fish Market one sturgeon weighs 120 pounds, and one swordfish weighs 36 pounds. If two halibut weigh the same as one swordfish what is the weight of one grouper, when the grouper and the swordfish together weigh as much as the sturgeon and the halibut?

ANSWER:

| Puzzle 12.15 | Difficulty rating: 4 |

NAILS

At the hardware store you can buy nails in boxes of six, nine, and twenty. What is the largest number of nails that it is not possible to obtain by purchasing some combination of boxes?

ANSWER:

FARMERS' MARKET

Karen went to the farmers' market to buy fruit. She ended up buying three boxes of fruit total, one full of cherries, one full of strawberries and one containing a mixture of both. The man who sold her the fruit put labels on the boxes but he was in a hurry and put the incorrect label on each box.

How can you label the boxes correctly if you are only allowed to take and look at just one piece of fruit from just one of the boxes?

ANSWER:

Puzzle 12.17	Difficulty rating: 4

PARADOX

You are in a room with two doors. Behind one door is a lion that will eat you if you open it and the second door will get you out of the room. There are two men in the room with you that know which door is the safe one. One of the two men always tells the truth and one of the men always tells lies. If you can only ask one of the men one question, what question could you ask that would give you the information you need to choose the correct door?

ANSWER:

EXPLOSION

Troy is an explosives expert who is wiring a cave to explode. He has 45 minutes to get out of the cave before it blows up but he doesn't have a watch. All he has are two fuses, each of which will burn up in exactly one hour. They are not of the same length and width as each other, so he can't measure a half hour by noting when one fuse is half burned. Using these two fuses, how can Troy measure 45 minutes?

ANSWER:

| Puzzle 12.19 | Difficulty rating: 4 |

COMPUTER KIT

Jerry goes to the mall to buy a mouse, keyboard and speakers for his computer. After some shopping around, he finds the best deals for each. The sum of the price of the speakers and six times the cost of the mouse minus three times the cost of the keyboard is $17. Also, four times the cost of the keyboard minus twice the cost of the speakers plus seven times the cost of the mouse is $13. In addition, 17 times what the keyboard costs plus 30 times what the mouse costs minus eight times the cost of the speakers totals $63. How much did Jerry spend at the mall?

ANSWER:

| Puzzle 12.20 | Difficulty rating: 4 |

Alberto is at the mall looking for a gift and sees a nice watch for $2. But thinking that it is too cheap to be any good, he finally sees one for more money that he really likes. He also sees a similar watch for his wife which costs the same. Alberto has $90 in his pocket. The money he has, together with five times the cost of his watch, times the cost of his wife's watch, minus the cost of 50 times the price of his wife's watch totals $45. Alberto buys both watches and then goes home. How much does Alberto have left after his shopping today?

ANSWER:

| Puzzle 12.21 | Difficulty rating: 4 |

BIRDBATH

You just bought a new birdbath, and it requires five gallons of water. You get out the garden hose to fill it, but because it needs to be exactly five gallons you go into your shed to find a measuring device. However, you only have a four-gallon bucket and a seven-gallon bucket. How can you accurately measure out five gallons for the birdbath?

ANSWER:

GRID PUZZLE

In the example grid the numbers all add up to 15, including diagonally. In the 4 x 4 grid below, if the box on the left contains the number 14, find the total for each of the rows.

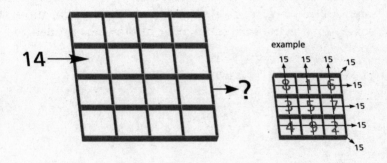

example

14 →

?

ANSWER:

MARBLES

Imagine that you have three boxes, one containing two black marbles, one containing two white marbles, and the third, one black marble and one white marble. The boxes were labeled for their contents – BB, WW and BW – but someone has switched the labels so that every box is now incorrectly labeled. You are allowed to take one marble at a time out of any box, without looking inside, and by this process of sampling you are to determine the contents of all three boxes. What is the smallest number of drawings needed to do this?

ANSWER:

| **Puzzle 12.24** | **Difficulty rating: 4** |

LAKE VIEW

A man is standing on a hill overlooking a calm lake. His eyes are 100 meters above the surface of the lake. He sees a balloon in the sky. He finds that the angle of elevation of the balloon is 30 degrees, and the angle of depression of the balloon's reflection in the lake is 60 degrees. What is the height of the balloon above the lake?

ANSWER:

| Puzzle 12.25 | Difficulty rating: 4 |

TUNNEL

A 0.5-kilometer-long train enters a tunnel that is 10 kilometers long. If the train is traveling at 35 kilometers per hour, how long will it take for the entire train to pass through the tunnel?

ANSWER:

HOUSE BUILDING

Tim owns a mason company and was hired to build a house. The entire house can be built in 31 days with five masons. Ten days after they started building the house, Tim hired 10 more masons to get the house built quicker. How many more days are required to finish the house?

ANSWER:

BACKGAMMON

The backgammon world championship took place in Monte Carlo. The tournament was organized in a round-robin format, with every participant playing a match against every other player once. If 105 matches were played in total, how many players were there in the tournament?

ANSWER:

ESCALATORS

Alberto likes going to the mall on weekends and running up the escalators. If he runs up eight steps of the escalator it takes him 33 seconds to reach the top. If he runs up 15 steps it only takes him 22.5 seconds to get to the top. How long would it take Alberto to reach the top if he didn't run up any steps?

ANSWER:

Puzzle 12.29	Difficulty rating: 4

FIND THE MISSING WORD

ml

750 →

1,500 →

3,000 →

6,000 →

9,000 →

?

12,000 →

ANSWER:

| Puzzle 12.30 | Difficulty rating: 4 |

489

LOLLIPOP TEASER

A teacher told her students, "I have a bag of lollipops that I bought for $6.25. Can anyone figure out how many are in the bag and how much I paid for each one?" The students looked puzzled and said there's no way anyone could know how many lollipops are in the bag. The teacher said, "The lollipops were all the same price. The number I bought is the same as the number of cents in each price." Can you figure out how much the lollipops cost?

ANSWER:

Puzzle 12.31	Difficulty rating: 4

DYNAMITE

You are in charge of building demolition and want to make sure you have enough time to get out of the building after lighting the fuses for the dynamite. All you know is that each fuse burns for one hour after lighting one end, but you need to time 45 minutes. With only two test fuses, how can you accurately measure the 45 minutes?

ANSWER:

| Puzzle 12.32 | Difficulty rating: 4 |

MISSING NUMBER

Can you work out what number should logically replace the question mark?

ANSWER:

STORM AHEAD

You are on vacation and want to charter a boat for the day. Concerned about possible bad weather, you ask the captain of the boat. The captain says the weather will be fine and he is correct two-thirds of the time. You check the national weather service, however, and they predict a bad storm. The national weather service has an impressive 75 per cent accuracy in predicting storms. What is the chance of a storm?

ANSWER:

| **Puzzle 12.34** | **Difficulty rating: 5** |

MARBLES

In front of you are two sacks of marbles. The first sack has 99 black marbles and one white marble, and the second sack has 99 white marbles and one black marble. You choose a sack randomly and take a single marble from it. If the marble is black, what is the probability that it was taken from the first sack with the 99 black marbles in it?

ANSWER:

CHOCOLATES

A box of chocolates can be divided equally among three, five or thirteen people. What is the smallest number of chocolates the box can contain?

ANSWER:

| Puzzle 12.36 | Difficulty rating: 4 |

Using a single cut (no more than two pieces) without lifting
your scissors from the sheet, transform figure A into figure B.

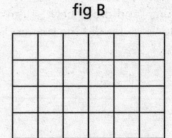

fig A

fig B

ANSWER:

ONWARD MARCH!

A column of soldiers one mile long is marching forward at a constant rate. The soldier at the front of the column has to deliver a message to the soldier at the rear. He breaks rank and begins marching toward the rear at a constant rate while the column continues forward. The soldier reaches the rear, delivers the message and immediately turns to march forward at a constant rate. When he reaches the front of the column and drops back in rank, the column has moved one mile. How far did the soldier delivering the message march?

ANSWER:

Puzzle 12.38	Difficulty rating: 5

CHAPTER 12 ANSWERS

12.1 10 $1 bills, 100 $5 bills, 9 $10 bills, and 18 $50 bills.

12.2 Five noodles. This one works well by working backward. On the last bite, the first person needs to eat between one and six noodles, so he can finish all the remaining noodles. The only way to guarantee this is if the other person has seven noodles to choose from. This means that on the next to last bite the opponent should be left with 14 noodles, 21 on the previous bite, and 28 and 35 on the bites previous to this. Therefore, the first person should take five noodles on his first bite and then base the number he takes on how many noodles his opponent eats each time.

12.3 Label the sacks from one to five. Take one coin out of sack one, and label it "1". Take two coins out of sack two, and label them both with a "2". Take three coins out of sack three, and label each with a "3". Continue this pattern with sacks four and five. Put these 15 coins on the tray of the scale. If all 15 weighed one pound, the scale would register 15 pounds, but since one or more of the coins weighs only nine-tenths of a pound, the scale will register less than 15. Subtract the number on the scale from 15. Your answer will tell you the number of the sack with the lighter coins. (If the scale registers 14.8 lbs, it's sack two. If the scale registers 14.5 lbs, it's sack five.)

12.4 420 students. This is the only number under 500 that can be divided evenly by 3, 4, 5 and 7.

12.5 336 miles. Day one he drove 84 miles. Day two he drove 126 miles. Day three he drove 94.5 miles. Day four he drove 10.5 miles, leaving 21 miles left to travel. 84 + 126 + 94.5 + 10.5 = 315 + 21 = 336.

12.6 The second store is the best option, on the assumption that Brian takes the ring back and buys it again at a later date. At the first store he spends $3,000 then returns to the same store and gets back $2,400; he buys again at $3,000 = $6,000 spent in total, which makes a net spend of $3,600. At the second store he spends $3,500 then returns and gets back $3,500; he buys again at $3,500 = $7,000 spent in total, which makes a net spend of $3,500.

12.7 The five football players will win. If there were only four football players on one side and two soccer players on the other side, it would be a tie.

12.8 80 miles. It took Vince four hours to get to Atlantic City going 20 miles an hour, and two hours to cover the distance at twice the speed (40 miles an hour).

12.9 Carlos picked 15.

12.10 Container E holds the apple juice. The second customer can buy twice as much as the first customer if the first customer buys Containers A and C (for a total of 66 quarts) and the second customer buys Containers B, D, and F (for a total of 132 quarts). The remaining container, E, must hold the apple juice.

12.11 Lauren is 5 foot 4 inches and Duncan is 6 foot.

12.12 b to g and

16 to 5
4-13
10-19
8-17
6-15
16-5
a-f
e-j
b-g
c-h

d-i
f-a
g-b
h-c
i-d
j-e
k-l
l-k

12.13 She drives 200 miles on the last day. If n = miles traveled in one day, let each subsequent day be n + 20 (the daily increase in miles). With this you'll find that she would travel 40 miles the first day, 60 the second day, 100 on the fourth day and 200 on the ninth and final day.

12.14 The number of possible seating arrangements is 6 x 5 x 4 x 3 x 2, which is 720. Therefore, they've been playing for 720 weeks or 13.8 years.

12.15 The grouper weighs 102 pounds. The weight of the halibut is given indirectly by saying two halibut weigh the same as one swordfish. One grouper and two halibut are equal to the weight of one sturgeon and one halibut. One grouper and one halibut must have the same weight as one sturgeon. So, the grouper is 120 pounds minus 18 pounds, or 102 pounds.

12.16 43 nails. 44 nails can be obtained with four boxes of six and a box of

20, and each combination at 44 and above can be achieved with the three box types listed.

12.17 Take a piece of fruit from the box marked "cherries and strawberries". If the fruit you take is a cherry, then that box must be the box containing just cherries (it can't be cherries and strawberries because we are told the labeling is incorrect). Therefore, the box marked "strawberries" can't be the box containing just cherries, and it can't be the box containing just strawberries either, so it must be the box containing cherries and strawberries. The remaining box is therefore the box containing just strawberries.

12.18 Ask one of the men what the other man would answer to the question, "Is the door on the left the correct door?" Then assume the answer you are given is false and act on that knowledge. If the man you ask is the liar, he'll incorrectly give you the truthful man's answer. If the man you ask is the truthful man, he'll correctly give you the liar's wrong answer.

12.19 Light one fuse at both ends and, at the same time, light the second fuse at one end. When the first fuse has completely burned, a half hour has elapsed and the second fuse has a half hour left to go. At this time, light the second fuse from the other end. This will cause it to burn out in 15 more minutes. At that point, exactly 45 minutes will have elapsed.

12.20 The speakers cost $14, the keyboard cost $5 and the mouse cost $3. Jerry spent $22.

12.21 He buys both watches for a total of $18, so he has $72 ($90 - $18) left.

12.22 You fill the four-gallon bucket and pour it into the seven-gallon one. Then you fill the four-gallon bucket a second time and pour it until the seven-gallon bucket is full, leaving one gallon left in the four-gallon bucket. Now, empty out the seven-gallon bucket, pour the one gallon of water from the four-gallon bucket into the larger bucket and fill the four-gallon bucket again, then pour the four gallons into the other bucket with the one gallon already in it. There you have five gallons!

12.23 34

1	8	12	13
14	11	7	2
15	10	6	3
4	5	9	16

12.24 You can learn the contents of all three boxes by drawing just one marble. The key to the solution is your knowledge that the labels on all three of the boxes are incorrect. You must draw a marble from the box labeled "black-white". Assume that the marble drawn is black. You know then that the other marble in this box must be black also, otherwise the label would be correct. Since you have now identified the box containing two black marbles, you can at once tell the contents of the box marked "white-white": you know it cannot contain two white marbles, because its label has to be wrong; it cannot contain two black marbles, for you have identified that box; therefore it must contain one black and one white marble. The third box, of course, must then be the one holding two white marbles. You can solve the puzzle by the same reasoning if the marble you draw from the "black-white" box happens to be white instead of black.

12.25 The balloon is 200 meters above the lake.

12.26 It will take the train 18 minutes. The front of the train has to initially travel 10 km to leave the tunnel, and then a further 0.5 km until the rear of the train has left the tunnel – a total of 10.5 km. Which takes 60 x (10.5 ÷ 35) = 18 minutes.

12.27 Seven days will finish the house. If it takes five masons 31 days, it would take ten masons 15.5 days to finish a house, and it would take 15 masons 10.3 days to complete a house. After ten days one-third of the house is built, so it takes the 15 masons 7 days to complete the remaining two-thirds of the project.

12.28 There were 15 players in the tournament. 14 + 13 +... + 2 + 1 = 105.

12.29 45 seconds. It takes 1.5 seconds per step so we find out there are 30 steps in total. 30 x 1.5 = 45.

12.30 Answer: Balthazar. Each of the numbers represent a wine bottle size, in ml. Bottle sizes: holds 750 ml – the standard size. Magnum: two bottles or 1.5 liters. Double Magnum: twice the size of a magnum, holding 3 liters, or the equivalent of 4 bottles. Imperial: holds 6 litres or the equivalent of 8 bottles. Salmanazar: holds 12 regular bottles (one case), or 9 liters. Balthazar: holds 16 bottles or 12 liters.

12.31 25 lollipops costing 25¢ each ($6.25 equals 625¢, and 625 divided by 25

= 25).

12.32 Take the two test fuses and light both ends of the first one and one end of the second one. After the first fuse has completely burnt, you will know that 30 minutes have passed, at which point light the other end of the second fuse, which will burn for 15 minutes, telling you when 45 minutes have passed.

12.33 The missing number is 16. The answer is found by dividing the number on the bottom by the number on the right and then squaring the result to find the number on the left.

12.34 60 per cent chance of a storm. The odds the captain is wrong is $1/3$ and the odds the weather service is right is $3/4$. $1/3 \times 3/4 = 1/4$. The odds the captain is right is $2/3$ and weather service is wrong is $1/4$. $2/3 \times 1/4 = 1/6$. Therefore, the probability of a storm is $1/4 \div (1/4 + 1/3) = 3/5$ or 60 per cent.

12.35 $99/100$. The probability that the sack with 99 black marbles is taken and 1 white marble is taken from that sack $= 1/2 \times 99/100 = 99/200$.
The probability that a white marble is taken $= (1/2 \times 99/100) + (1/2 \times 1/100) = 100/200 = 1/2$.
Therefore we get $(99/200) \div (100/200) = 99/100$.

12.36 195

12.37

fig A   fig B

12.38 2.4 miles.
Let r1 = rate of the column = 1 mile/hr. Let r2 = rate of the messenger. d = distance covered by messenger. t = time to move one mile = 1 hour. The meeting point of the messenger and the person at the rear is a distance of $r2 \div (1 + r2)$ from the starting point of the messenger. This is just the ratio of the messenger's rate divided by the sum of the two rates. The messenger will have to cover the distance to the meeting point, turn around and cover it again, and then march one more mile. So...
$d = 2 \times r2 \div (1 + r2)$.
distance = rate x time, so...
$2 \times r2 \div (1 + r2) = r2 \times 1$
$2 \times r2 \div (1 + r2) = r2 - 1$
$2 \times r2 = r22 - 1$
$r22 - 2 \times r2 - 1 = 0$
Use the quadratic equation to solve for r2...
$r2 = (2 + 81/2) \div 2 = 1 + 21/2 = \sim$ 2.4142 miles/hr
Since he is marching for one hour the distance is 2.4142 miles.

502